n West

Quebec
Montreal
MAINE
VERMONT
N.H.
Boston
MASS.
Plymouth Rock
CONN.
IROQUOIS
NEW YORK
New York
PENNSYLVANIA
N.J.
DELAWARES
Philadelphia
MARYLAND
Baltimore
POWATANS
Jamestown
W. VIRGINIA
VIRGINIA
N. CAROLINA
New Bern
S. CAROLINA
GEORGIA
CREEK
Savannah
FLORIDA
ALABAMA
CHEROKEE
TENNESSEE
KENTUCKY
Boonesboro
NEUTRALS
OHIO
SHAWNEE
INDIANA
ILLINOIS
ILLINOIS
Nauvoo
MICHIGAN
HURON
Fort Michilmackinac
Green Bay
WISCONSIN
Falls of St Anthony
St. Louis
Cahokia
Independence
MISSOURI
ARKANSAS
Fort Smith
Little Rock
Mississippi
MISSISSIPPI
LOUISIANA
New Orleans

W9-CAX-690

THE COLORFUL STORY OF
THE AMERICAN
WEST

THE COLORFUL STORY OF THE AMERICAN WEST

Royal B Hassrick

OCTOPUS

First published 1975 by Octopus Books Limited
59 Grosvenor Street, London W 1
ISBN 0 7064 0420 3
© 1975 Octopus Books Limited
Distributed in Australia by Rigby Limited
30 North Terrace, Kent Town, Adelaide
South Australia 5067
Produced by Mandarin Publishers Limited
Westlands Road, Quarry Bay, Hong Kong
Printed in Hong Kong

CONTENTS

THE EXPLORERS & COLONISTS

The discovery of America was to open the floodgates of Europe to those who came in search of Indian gold and territories to claim in the name of God and their homelands.

Below *Christopher Columbus* by Sebastiono de Piombo
Right *The Rocky Mountains* by James Lanmon

THE HISTORY of the American West is in reality the saga of many men, courageous, enterprising, sometimes desperate men, who together believed in and hewed out a most dramatic national destiny. That it was accomplished in large measure as a matter of life and death was of significant importance. The rewards were worth the risks and as such they proved to be the making of one of history's most brilliantly successful gambles. The actors on this stage thought in terms of survival and escape, wealth and freedom, and to these goals they spent their energies, their wits and often their very lives. The story of their ambitions is the key to an American heritage ablaze with valor and color. There had been nothing quite like it before and there will never be anything quite like it again.

It all began with an ingenious theory of Christopher Columbus. He thought the world was round and believed that by sailing west he could more easily reach the rich ports of India and the Orient. Having successfully convinced Queen Isabella of Spain that the idea was practical he made a slight and understandable miscalculation and never reached India. The Spaniards however capitalized upon his western discovery. It proved to be a fabulous windfall. Under the valiant leadership of men like Cortez and Pizarro, the Spanish conquered the mysterious and majestic New World civilizations of the Aztecs and Incas. So complete was the conquest that they not only plundered the victims of their wealth in gold and imposed on the natives the avid proselytizing of the Franciscan Fathers, but also plunged them into slavery. To those Indians who proved recalcitrant, the Spanish went to the extremes of cutting off their hands and feet to convince them of Christianity's omnipotence. Then and there the Spaniards, as ruthless, robbing bigots, set the stage for the development of the American West.

As early as 1513, Juan Ponce de Leon, seeking the Fountain of Youth, made his first voyage to Florida. Later in 1521 he was commissioned to conquer the "Isle of Florida" in the name of Spain. With two hundred men, fifty horses and farm implements, he set out from Puerto Rico in two ships. Reaching the West Coast, his party was savagely attacked by Indians. Instead of finding the "Fountain," cocky Ponce was deservedly shot in the back by a poisoned arrow. Turning his expedition around, he headed for Cuba where he shortly afterwards died.

It was a black Moroccan named Estevanico who in the spring of 1539 was the first foreigner to enter the Southwest. Leading an army of three hundred Indian soldiers from Mexico, this pompous Spanish slave reached the Zuni pueblo of Hawikuh. There he immediately demanded tribute in turquoise and women. Haughtily he announced that white men were following three days behind. The Zuni elders, having deliberated as was their custom, decided unanimously that they wanted no part of Estevanico or his demands. The Zunis, instead, shot the arrogant Moor through with arrows. The Mexican survivors fled toward home, taking with them the white men and their frightened friars.

Above A woodcut showing conquistadors attacking an Indian village
Right Francisco Vásquez de Coronado in the summer of 1540 gave the Zuni Indians a taste of Spanish steel. The Indians were no match for mounted troops and gunpowder

The following summer Don Francisco Vásquez de Coronado, lured by the imagined wealth of the fabled Seven Cities of Cibola, arrived in the land of the Zunis. With him he brought mounted soldiers astride horses, beasts the Zunis had never seen. When the Zunis refused to submit to the Spaniard's imperious demands, Coronado attacked. The Indians retaliated, shooting arrows and throwing stones. They dented Coronado's shining helmet with so many rocks that the conquistador was at first dragged away for dead. In less than an hour, however, the Zunis were subdued.

By September of the same year, more of Coronado's troops arrived, together with an entourage of cattle, sheep, swine and horses. Besides the troops, there were also white men, women and children. In no time these interlopers usurped the land of the Pueblos. They commandeered their dwellings, their food, even their women, and subjected the Indian men to the kind of slavery in which the Spanish were specialists.

Coronado was both greedy and restless. The Cities of Cibola proved disappointing. Looting the Pueblos yielded nothing whatsoever by way of riches. The Indians simply had no gold. But tantalizing rumors

Left *Buffalo Crossing the Yellowstone* by Charles Wimar. Millions of these massive beasts roamed the Plains prior to their wanton slaughter by the white man in the mid-19th century
Top *The Wild Turkey* by John James Audubon. English colonists feasted on four turkeys at their first Thanksgiving celebration
Above The splendors of the West, typified in Thomas Moran's *Western Landscape*, were not fully revealed until the turn of the 19th century

reached the Spaniards of fabulous wealth to be found to the northeast. So in the summer of 1541 Coronado set out for Quivira, a grueling expedition guided by a Plains Indian called the Turk. When they finally reached the dry flats of what is now southwestern Oklahoma and Kansas, however, all they found were the grass lodges of the Wichita Indians or Pawnee Picts. The golden cities of Quivira were equally a myth. Disillusioned, Coronado at last gave up. He turned around, collected his hogs and horses, his cattle and people and returned thoroughly disheartened to Mexico.

The Spaniards, however, were as hard to discourage as a swarm of hornets determined to build a nest. Forty years later they returned to the shimmering desert lands of the Pueblos, four-hundred strong, bringing over seven thousand rooting hogs and smelly sheep, bellowing cattle and rambunctious horses. Led by a villainous governor, Don Juan de Oñate, they subjugated the Pueblos, taking special vengeance on the Acomas at Sky City who had dared to resist. Oñate ordered that those Indian men he didn't kill, should have one foot chopped off. Then he herded them into slavery for twenty years. Women and children were given slightly lesser terms.

By now the Spaniards had planted their colony firmly, or so they thought, building their dried mud capital at Santa Fe. Here and there they set their little rancheros along the rivers which cut the land of towering mesas and rugged canyons. Franciscan friars in their somber black robes invaded the Pueblos, Taos and Picuris, San Ildefonso, Hemez and San Felipe, brought Christianity to the heathens, added souls to the Catholic Church and strove to abolish the worship of the evil gods the Indians revered. This was as presumptuous as it was tragic. The Pueblos had been living in peace for hundreds of years. To impose an alien faith, even if brought to man by the Prince of Peace, was altogether inhumane.

This Spanish domination, whereby they established their haciendas and enriched themselves by the labors of the Indian serfs, lasted nearly a century. And then one summer's day in 1680 the Pueblos arose. Led by Popé, a man from San Juan who had brooded and schemed during his years in prison at Santa Fe, the Indians joined forces. They attacked the rancheros, the tiny settlements, the capital itself. Enraged, they drove from their homes some twenty-five hundred Spaniards, including the governor from his adobe palace. Nearly five hundred settlers were killed as were many of the friars. With this swift and telling revolt, the Spanish colonial control of the Southwest was temporarily ended. The conquerors had been given a little taste of their own savagery.

Much earlier, Hernando de Soto was authorized by Spain's Charles V to conquer Florida, which really meant the entire continent of North America. His mission was to search for gold and precious stones and to claim the land for Spain. Landing in Florida in 1539, the conquistador marched his men north through Georgia to what now is Tennessee, then southwest to

Far left The English explorer John Smith was one of the founders of the colony of Virginia
Left The Indian princess Pocahontas saved John Smith's life. This portrait dates from her later years in London as a court favorite
Above *The Murder of David Tulley's Family*, a painting by Peter Rindisbacher. The early settlers lived under constant threat of Indian attack

Alabama. Here in one of his many ruthless engagements with the Indians, he was wounded. Undaunted, he pressed westward, crossed the Mississippi and trekked up the Arkansas River as far as Oklahoma. Finding no treasure, he gave up and turned south, making his way back to the Mississippi. Here he died of his wounds and was buried in the river. His men traveled on, finally reaching Vera Cruz in 1543. Despite his untimely demise—he was only forty-two years old—de Soto's trip was monumental. He had explored more of North America than any other European. Like Coronado, he had found no wealth, had, indeed, ended his expedition in financial ruin. It would seem, on occasion, that lust for other people's property, land and lives brings its own retribution.

When the first English colonists landed in 1607 at what was to become Jamestown, Virginia, there was no real concept of an American West. At first the Indians welcomed the white men, even to the extent of bringing them life-sustaining foods when the colonists' faltering crops failed and famine was imminent. A timorous alliance was even formed with the marriage of the Indian princess, Pocahontas, to the Englishman, John Rolfe. However, with her sudden death in England at the age of twenty-one and that of her father, the ruling Powhatan, a year later in 1618, old wounds reopened. In 1622 the Indians savagely attacked the colony, reducing its numbers to a mere three hundred and fifty souls. In retaliation, the English mustered a small army and by 1650 had destroyed all Indian resistance to white encroachment. The Englishman's foothold in the New World would now be secure.

As with the Jamestown colonists, so it was with the Massachusetts settlers. Landing at Plymouth Rock in 1620, they, too, were welcomed by the Indians. The following year the struggling Pilgrims, who had been instructed in the planting of crops, celebrated with neighboring Indians their first Thanksgiving. With a harvest they had raised, added to what the Indians contributed, they also feasted on four wild turkeys. But as this and other English colonies prospered throughout New England, friction developed. Fearing an attack, Miles Standish marched against the Indians as early as 1623. Peace was made with Massasoit, chief of the Wampanoag, which lasted fifty years, but that was most unusual. The Indians and the colonists clashed again and again. The result was that the Indians were gradually driven from their lands. The pattern for American's westward expansion was already being set.

The French also arrived early, establishing their principal settlements along the St. Lawrence River.

Unlike the Spanish explorers who were searching for treasure, the French were seeking trade routes. Robert Cavelier, sieur de La Salle, commandant of Fort Frontenac, began building forts as far west as the Great Lakes to protect his fur-trading interests. On an expedition beginning in 1679, he took with him Father Louis Hennepin as official friar, Michel Aco, his lieutenant, and Henri de Tonti. They sailed the Great Lakes in the *Griffon*, in which they reached Green Bay, Wisconsin. Proceeding further, they came to the Illinois River where La Salle built Fort Creve Coeur.

Below One of the earliest seekers of the Northwest Passage was Alexander Mackenzie, portrayed here by Thomas Lawrence. He gave his name to what is now the Mackenzie River but failed in his main objective although he tried several routes

Right This map by Thomas Kitchen, dated 1763 shows the extent of British Dominions in America at that time. It also shows the extent to which America was still relatively unexplored

Here La Salle split his party, sending Hennepin and Aco to explore the upper Mississippi while he returned to Fort Frontenac for supplies. Hennepin and Aco were soon captured by Sioux Indians, but did discover the Falls of St. Anthony, the site of St. Paul-Minneapolis, Minnesota.

Daniel Greysolon, sieur Duluth, was already in the West settling a conflict between the warring Ojibway and Sioux. At Mille Lacs, Minnesota, he claimed the upper Mississippi for France. In addition to establishing his fur-trading interests, he was searching for a northwest passage, a waterway to the Pacific. His plans, however, were temporarily interrupted by the need to rescue Father Hennepin and Michel Aco from the Sioux. In this, as was true of most of his endeavors, his diplomacy proved entirely successful. He then returned to his main ambition that of seeking a northwest passage. Not finding one represented to him a major failure.

Meanwhile, La Salle was making plans for an equally

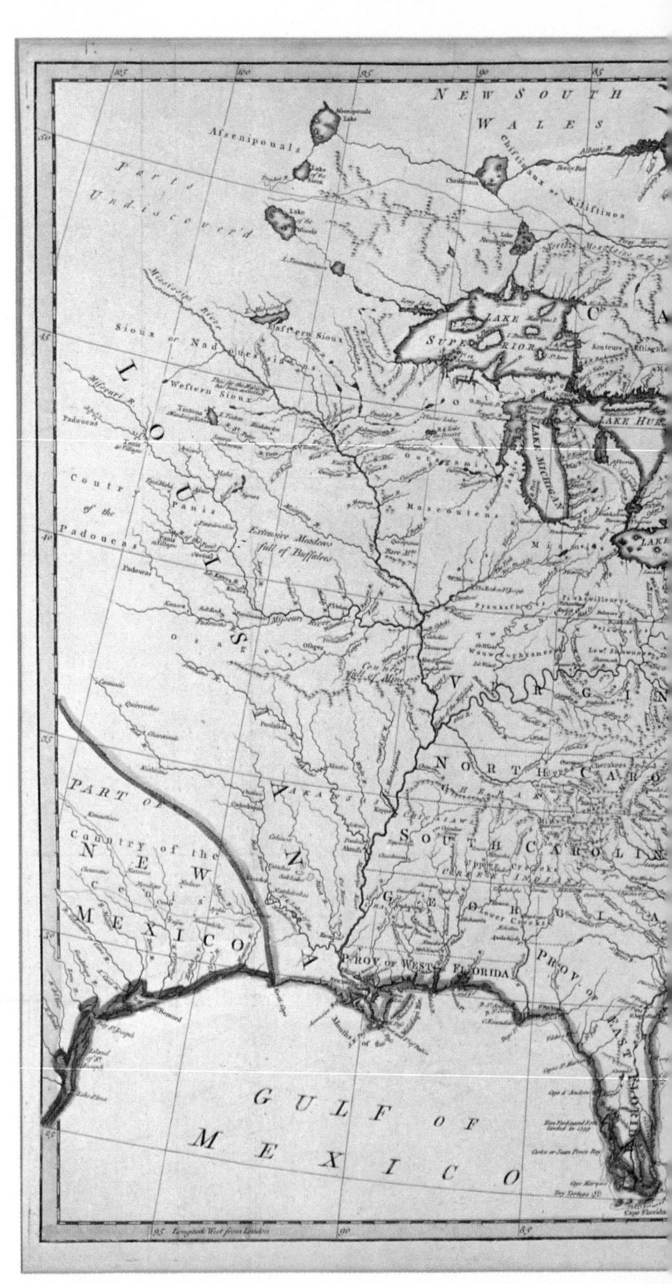

ambitious venture, that of finding the mouth of the Mississippi River. Unlike Duluth, who in truth was at a dead end since all the waters he faced were upstream, La Salle could reason with confidence that if he headed downstream, the Great Muddy River would surely have an outlet. Together with Tonti, La Salle set out from Mackinac Island and ended up at the Gulf of Mexico in the spring of 1682. Here he proclaimed all of Louisiana in the name of France. Some years later he undertook an expedition to the gulf by sea designed to consolidate France's claim more firmly. Although one of his ships sank and another was captured by the Spanish, he managed to reach shore. But he could not find the Mississippi's delta, much less the river. As he was trekking inland in a frantic search, his men finally mutinied and La Salle was murdered, a sad end to one of France's and America's most gallant cavaliers.

The Spanish and French were not the only explorers. The English, too, were avidly searching the country, especially for a northwest passage. Alexander Mackenzie was one of the more resolute. Troubled by the expense, distance and difficulties of transporting furs from the far Northwest to his North West Fur Company in Montreal, he determined to find a navigable passage to the Pacific. Linking the beaver trade with that of the Pacific sea otter would prove more profitable. Mackenzie had searched for the route earlier. By following what is now the Mackenzie River to its mouth, he was poorly rewarded by reaching the Arctic Ocean. Now he would try another route. Leaving Lake Athabasca in the spring of 1793, he embarked on the Peace River in a canoe. Crossing the Continental Divide—a portage of less than a mile—he shot down the Frazer River, climbed several mountains and finally, on the Bella Cola River, reached the Pacific north of Vancouver Island. Then and there he realized the route was impractical. His journey, however, combined with Captain James Cook's explorations, made secure the British grip on western Canada.

A NEW and ACCURATE MAP of the BRITISH DOMINIONS in AMERICA, according to the Treaty of 1763: Divided into the several PROVINCES and JURISDICTIONS. Projected upon the best AUTHORITIES and Astronomical Observations. By Tho. Kitchin Geographer.

Below Indian massacres were grim realities of frontier life. This vivid painting by John Vanderlyn is entitled *The Murder of Jane McCrea*. Shawnees attacked the settlements of western Pennsylvania while Iroquois burned and pillaged the upper New York region. The result was that treaties were ignored and when Indian vengeance showed itself the whole process was repeated. It is little wonder that in the eyes of the settler the only good Indian was a dead one

So it was as other colonies were formed. The Dutch in 1624 reached the mouth of the Hudson River and a year later named their settlement New Amsterdam. Farther south along the shores of the Delaware, the Swedes set their towns. Penn's Pennsylvania and Oglethorpe's Georgia lured men and women to the opportunities of the New World.

From England and Germany, from France and North

Meriwether Lewis *Thomas Jefferson* *William Clark*

Ireland, first in driblets, then in droves, the colonists arrived. They sought their fortunes as coopers and blacksmiths, as millers and farmers. Within a century the feebly struggling settlements at Jamestown and Plymouth had grown into established cities. Savannah, in Georgia, New Bern in North Carolina, and Williamsburg in Virginia, all became important urban centers. By 1730 Philadelphia was the largest colonial capital with a population of forty thousand, while Baltimore, New York, Providence and Boston were also thriving towns.

In large measure the prospering of these cities as centers of commerce was thanks to the growing agricultural economy of the colonies. By the mid-eighteenth century, German immigrants had well-secured farming communities north along the Hudson River. Germans and men from the north of Ireland, referred to as "Scotch-Irish", had already pushed into western Pennsylvania and down the Cumberland valley, hard against the barrier of the Appalachian Mountains. Englishmen from Virginia were also hewing their way west, chopping out little clearings. Like the New Yorkers of the Hudson and Pennsylvanians of Lancaster County, theirs was a life of mere existence, one of felling trees, of building rude log cabins, of grubbing a few acres for a meager crop of corn and potatoes and beans.

In a sense, these pioneers were people with their backs against a wall. Their very desperation demanded a courage and industriousness which in reality saved them. In addition to the arduous work for sheer survival, they had to contend with the ever-present threat of attack by Indians.

Opposite Karl Bodmer's painting of a Mandan village on the banks of the Missouri River where Lewis and Clark spent their first winter
Top *Into the Unknown* by J.K. Ralston. Lewis and Clark meet the Shoshoni Indians
Above A Blackfeet Indian Chief, painting by Karl Bodmer. Lewis and Clark clashed with Blackfeet on their return journey

During both the drawn-out French and Indian wars as well as the American Revolution, the frontier was awash with blood. The French and the English each made alliances with the Indians, much to the alarm of the struggling farmers. A vicious raid by the French against the little town of Deerfield in 1704 nearly destroyed the village. Led by Hutel de Rouville, fifty Frenchmen and two hundred Abenaki and Christian Indians ravished the town. Killing fifty-three men, women and children, they marched over a hundred in to captivity in Canada. John Butler with a party of Indians and Tories perpetrated a similar massacre on the Wyoming Valley settlements in Pennsylvania in 1778.

The Indian scourge was constant in the West. Shawnees attacked the settlements of western Pennsylvania while Iroquois burned and pillaged the upper New York regions. So incensed did the Americans become that in the spring of 1779 General George Washington ordered an expedition under the command of General John Sullivan to eradicate the Indian menace. Leading a large army of Continentals to the Iroquois villages, by summer's end he had completely destroyed them. And with this brilliant conquest, the power of the Iroquois was forever broken.

At the end of the Revolution, such young states as Georgia, the Carolinas, Virginia and Pennsylvania, all of which possessed western borders, were finding it especially difficult to restrain the western migration of their citizens. In the Greenville Treaty of 1795 with such tribes as the Wyandot and Shawnee, the Piankeshaw and Delaware, a line was drawn beyond which the white man might not go. But arbitrary and imaginary lines agreed upon by far-off diplomats were meaningless to rude and hardy frontiersmen. They argued that the Indians didn't use the land except for hunting, besides which, as a treacherous menace, they should really be eliminated anyway. To a lone settler in the wilderness, the best Indian was a dead Indian. And with that theory for support, the westerners disregarded the treaty and breached the line. As squatters, they boldly cleared the forests and set up their little farms. As often as not they drew the wrath of the Indians who retaliated by burning their cabins and scalping the trespassers. It was a conflict that was to last for a century and a half.

Thomas Jefferson, third President of the United States, was well aware of the pressures upon the nation for expansion. British domination of the territories north and west of the Great Lakes and Spanish control of that vast and unknown region west of the Mississippi called Louisiana posed a threat to a struggling nation, a nation that was bursting at the seams.

Whether the thought of military conquest of Louisiana ever entered Jefferson's mind will probably never be known. He did, however, in 1803, enlist the services of young Meriwether Lewis to make an exploratory expedition to Louisiana with the object of ascertaining Spanish strength in the area and of discovering a practical water route to the Pacific. The President, furthermore, got Congress to appropriate funds for the ostensible purpose of extending United States commerce.

Captain Lewis recruited Captain William Clark to be his lieutenant and then promptly began making preparations for the journey. At the time, it was planned as little more than an outright spying mission. But then, fortuitously, a major upset in world events took place. Napoleon Bonaparte, who had accepted Louisiana from Spain in a treaty of 1800, found himself in dire financial difficulties. His warlike ambitions were costing France more than she could afford. Alert to this situation, Jefferson boldly sent emissaries to France with an offer of ten thousand dollars to purchase New Orleans and Florida. New Orleans was an area vital to American trade on the Mississippi and one which the Spaniards as toll collectors had always made a bottleneck. When the American diplomats arrived in France and made their proposal to the French, they were startled out of their lace shirts by the negotiator's counter offer—fifteen million dollars for the whole of Louisiana. Hastily the Americans sent for instructions. When James Monroe arrived as Jefferson's new envoy, he risked the bargain and bought nearly ten thousand square miles of wilderness. At four cents an acre, the 'Louisiana Purchase' was a dazzling buy.

Lewis and Clark's preparations had proceeded with dispatch. A notable addition to their equipment now, however, was a supply of American flags and silver Peace Medals with which to impress the Indians as they entered the newly acquired territory. Now they would come as official representatives of the United States. This was assuredly better than skulking around like a couple of spies.

On May 14, 1804, leaving Kahoka near St. Louis, with a party of thirty frontiersmen and hardened army men recruited from western posts, they started up the Missouri River in a fifty-five-foot keelboat fitted with a sail and two wooden canoes. Laboriously they worried their way up the river. The sail proved to be mostly for appearance, so they poled and towed their way.

As they progressed, the officers conferred with Indian tribes they met along the route. Lewis and Clark were careful to inform them that their allegiance from now on was to be to the United States. To confirm that relationship, they doled out beads and ribbons and Peace Medals. All went well until they encountered the Sioux near the Bad River. The Indians were more than delighted with the gifts, but soon became surly and overbearing. The Sioux had no intention of permitting white men to open trade negotiations with their Indian enemies farther upriver. The Sioux feigned drunkenness, would not leave the boat and at one point one headman boisterously insulted Lewis with such lewd and suggestive gestures that the captain was, in his own words, "forced to draw my sword."

By November the party had reached the Mandan villages perched high on the banks of the Missouri. These Indians lived in great earth lodges along the northern reaches of the river in what is now North Dakota. Here Lewis and Clark decided to set up winter camp. Here they trained their men and refurbished their equipment. It was here also that they persuaded Charbonneau, the trader, to serve as an interpreter and to bring with him his young Shoshoni wife, Sacagawea. Having earlier been captured by the Hidatsa, she knew her way back to the Rocky Mountains.

By April 7 the explorers were ready. Again they rowed and poled and tugged their overladen canoes and pirogues against the current of the river. And then, after their portage at the Great Falls of the Missouri, a decision had to be reached. It was now necessary to determine which of three rivers—the Jefferson, the Gallatin or the Madison—offered the best passage to the West. It turned out that the Jefferson was the one. Sacagawea reassured the party by recognizing the scenery. Proceeding up the Beaverhead River, they crossed the Continental Divide and traversed the mountains by the Lemhi Pass to the land of the Shoshonis. It was here the explorers hoped to obtain horses. Without these animals their trek to the Pacific would be almost impossible. The first meeting with a band of Shoshoni was a wary confrontation, but everything was soon happily resolved when it transpired that the Shoshoni chief was in fact the brother of Sacagawea. With that bit of good fortune, the expedition was provided with horses and continued its course.

Above La Salle's second expedition to the gulf was dogged by bad luck. His men finally mutinied and murdered him

The trip through the Rocky Mountain region was arduous and especially telling. While Lewis and Clark were well aware of the mountains' existence, they had no idea whatsoever of their extent. Instead of one range, there were many. And between then were vast stretches of barren and inhospitable plateau land. When at last the expedition reached the Clearwater River, they abandoned their horses. Making new canoes, they were rushed down the surging torrents of the Clearwater, Snake and Columbia rivers until they were poured out into the Pacific. Arriving on November 7, 1805, they made plans to build a small fort in the vicinity. They named it Clatsop and spent a very wet and miserable winter, much like bedraggled muskrats in an overflooded pond. An annual average rainfall of over a hundred and twenty inches is something to be coped with. The Lewis and Clark party were up to it.

After some five months of building, of preparing notes and establishing a claim for the United States to the region, the explorers began their return. They followed their original route over the hazardous Cascade Mountains until they reached the Nez Percé villages, where they picked up their horses. At the forks of the Bitterroot they split their forces, Lewis heading east over the Lewis and Clark Pass. Near Great Falls he explored the Marias River, hoping to find a western waterway. There was none. On his return to rendezvous with Clark, who had turned south and east to follow the Yellowstone River to its junction with the Missouri, Lewis was confronted by Blackfeet Indians. Parleying, the Indians insisted on making camp with the party. While Lewis slept, the Blackfeet tried to steal his gun and his horses. Awakening, the explorers pursued the Indians, killed two and then hastily retreated down the river to safety. Lewis and his men were badly outnumbered and could easily have been massacred. Sleeping with the enemy in camp was one of the few mistakes Lewis committed and he was lucky it cost him no dearer.

Lewis joined Clark below the forks of the Yellowstone on August 12, 1806. Together they reached the Mandan villages on the fifteen and were welcomed in St. Louis a month later. Their mission had been a complete success. They had failed to find a Northwest Passage, it is true. There wasn't one. What they had done was to dispel a myth. But they had established the United States' claim to the Northwest, they had informed the Indians and the fur traders that henceforth their allegiance was to be to the new nation, and finally, they had compiled copious and valuable information about the nation's vast new territory, Louisiana.

Lewis and Clark were not the only government explorers of the nation's new acquisition. Zebulon Pike surveyed the land along the southern Rockies and got himself captured by Spanish troops for trespassing. Stephen Long made several explorations throughout the territory, some of which yielded impressive scientific information. Later a man named Frémont would make history with his discoveries. It was through the fortitude of these men and those before them that the building of the West could begin, for it was they who opened the vistas and unveiled the mysteries of a fabulous new empire.

THE FUR TRADERS

Contact with the Indians proved profitable. Trading posts were set up for the exchange of furs for hardware and trinkets. White trappers were soon on the scene, fanning out north and westwards in their search for the beaver and the bear.

Above A sketch of a fur trapper by Frederic Remington
Right *Trapping Beaver* by Jacob Miller

THE BUILDING of the West was motivated as much by the prospect of exploitation as it was by the thought of agricultural production. In the Spanish Southwest, gold and fabulous jewels were the lure. Far to the northwest along the St. Lawrence River, fur was the magnet. The French and the English were quick to capitalize. As early as 1668, the Hudson's Bay Company was formed to help meet the insatiable European market.

From Quebec and Montreal, traders set their sights on Hudson's Bay and the Great Lakes to tap the wealth. In return for beads and blankets, for metal tools, firearms and whiskey, the Indians gathered huge quantities of precious pelts. Fort Michilimackinac, an island at the northwest tip of Lake Huron, became the principal trading center in the latter part of the eighteenth Century. Here French voyageurs loaded their ninety-pound bales of furs into birchbark canoes to paddle and portage nearly two thousand miles to Montreal. With luck they could make it in less than a fortnight. The French traders seemed to have an innate flair for living in the wilderness. Unlike the English, who considered the woods and forests as obstacles to be chopped down and the Indians as savages blocking the way to desirable land, the French discovered the forests to be a source of wealth and the Indians to be essential partners in a mutually profitable enterprise. In many instances they learned the language and more often than not took an Indian woman as a wife. And with this attitude, the French made the fur trade flourish.

A wide variety of furs were in demand, especially the desirable mink and otter, fox and beaver. But the skins of the bear, the deer, the elk and the buffalo sold well as robes and hides. After the treaty of 1763 when the British gained firm control of France's Canadian territories, companies like the North West, organized in 1779, spread their factories or trading posts throughout the Northwest. Scotsmen and Englishmen headquartered in Montreal hired the experienced French *coureurs de bois* to manage their western posts. They now controlled stations as far west as Vincennes, Kaskaskia and Kahoka and their traders ranged from the Pawnee country throughout much of Louisiana east of the Rockies. To the north lay the territory of the Hudson's Bay Company. With profits high and competition stiff, conflict between the two companies was intense. Furs were stolen, Indian tribes were pitted against one another and bribes in the form of excess whiskey were commonplace. Not until 1811 was a settlement reached and finally resolved by the Hudson's Bay Company absorbing the North West.

After the Revolution, the Americans determined to

enter the lucrative business so long dominated by the British. Traders were licensed with provisos that no credit be extended and that no liquor be sold lest the Indians be demoralized. The idea was naïve on both counts and failed brilliantly. The effective way to trade was to offer the Indians beads and tobacco, mirrors and guns, salt and ammunition and great quantities of whiskey. All these were exchanged at a high rate in return for furs at a low one. The unit of value was the highly prized skin of the castor or beaver. By disregarding the arbitrary regulations, the Americans soon began to challenge the British monopoly.

John Jacob Astor, born in Germany in 1763, came to New York at the age of twenty. After a stint as a baker's helper, he found employment with a fur merchant. Quickly learning the fundamentals of that business, Astor set up on his own. His idea was to capitalize first on procuring furs from New York State, Canada, and by 1800, the Great Lakes region. Trade in furs with China was now profitable. Soon Astor acquired his own ships and with this advantage was shortly counted among the wealthiest men in the United States. With the Louisiana Purchase, it occurred to him that this region would make a pleasant monopoly. In 1808 he formed the American Fur Company and later the Pacific Fur Company to handle the Far West business.

Below *Indians Bartering* by Coke Smith. Traders made vast profits by purchasing furs in exchange for textiles and firearms
Bottom *Blackfeet Encampment* by Karl Bodmer. Fur trappers were frequently attacked and killed by Indians

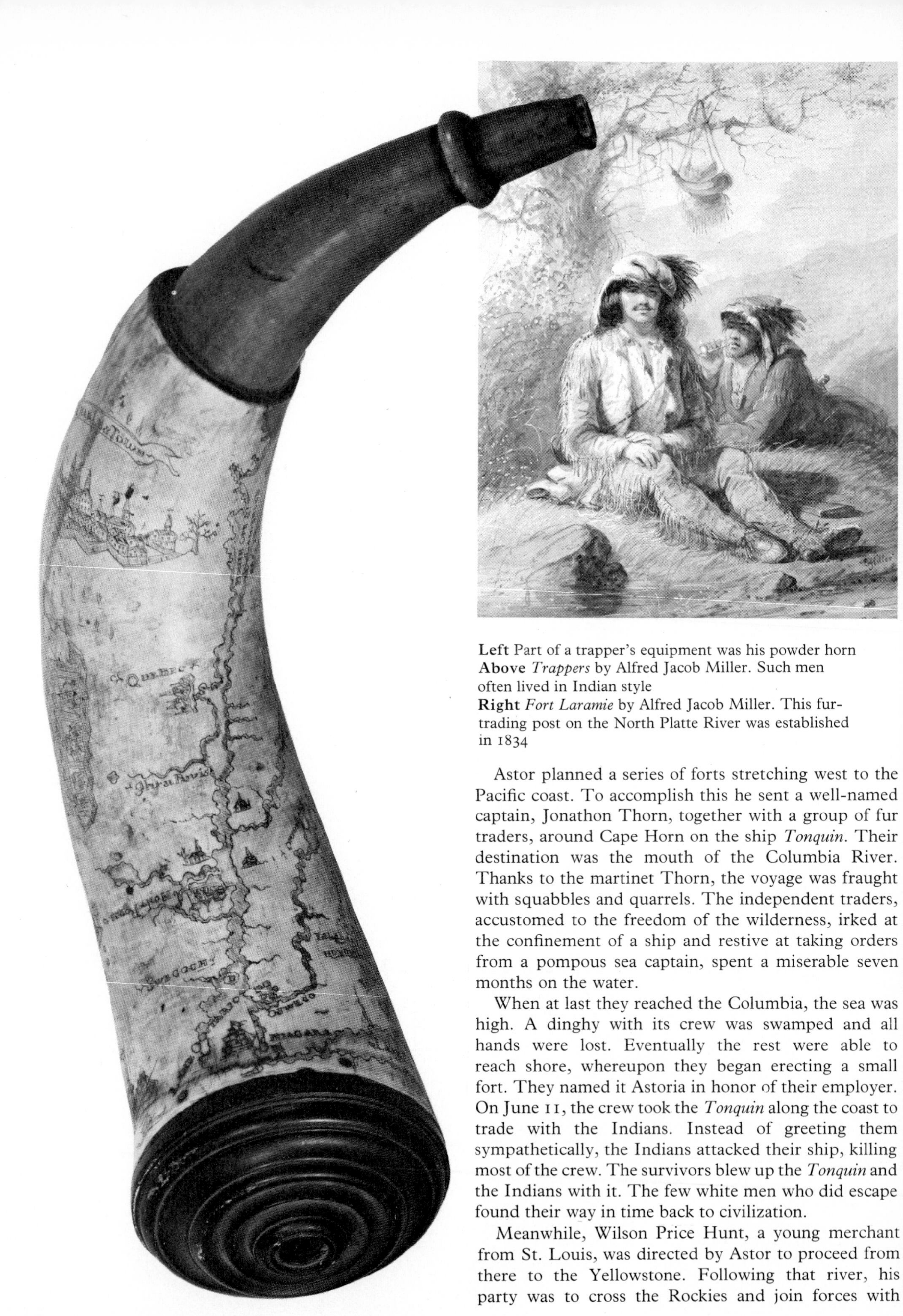

Left Part of a trapper's equipment was his powder horn
Above *Trappers* by Alfred Jacob Miller. Such men often lived in Indian style
Right *Fort Laramie* by Alfred Jacob Miller. This fur-trading post on the North Platte River was established in 1834

Astor planned a series of forts stretching west to the Pacific coast. To accomplish this he sent a well-named captain, Jonathon Thorn, together with a group of fur traders, around Cape Horn on the ship *Tonquin*. Their destination was the mouth of the Columbia River. Thanks to the martinet Thorn, the voyage was fraught with squabbles and quarrels. The independent traders, accustomed to the freedom of the wilderness, irked at the confinement of a ship and restive at taking orders from a pompous sea captain, spent a miserable seven months on the water.

When at last they reached the Columbia, the sea was high. A dinghy with its crew was swamped and all hands were lost. Eventually the rest were able to reach shore, whereupon they began erecting a small fort. They named it Astoria in honor of their employer. On June 11, the crew took the *Tonquin* along the coast to trade with the Indians. Instead of greeting them sympathetically, the Indians attacked their ship, killing most of the crew. The survivors blew up the *Tonquin* and the Indians with it. The few white men who did escape found their way in time back to civilization.

Meanwhile, Wilson Price Hunt, a young merchant from St. Louis, was directed by Astor to proceed from there to the Yellowstone. Following that river, his party was to cross the Rockies and join forces with

Thorn on the coast. But as Hunt's party moved farther up the Missouri, they became alarmed. Manuel Lisa, the fur trader, warned of the rapaciousness of the Blackfeet. Rather than travel along the Yellowstone, Hunt changed his course for one due west, traversing the Plains to the Black Hills of South Dakota. From here the men continued west, crossed the Big Horn River and once over Teton Pass reached the Snake. Their intention was to coast down the river in canoes until they reached the mountains. But the waters in the deep canyons were roily. Canoes sank, one man was lost. Deciding the party was so large as to be cumbersome when crossing the Cascades, Hunt divided his men into four groups. And then the troubles really began. The mountains were almost impassable, provisions dwindled, intense cold and deep snow hampered progress. Some men deserted, and some men died. Not until January, 1812, did the first party arrive at the fort. Hunt's own detachment appeared in February, the final group not until May.

No sooner had they reached the safety of Astoria than a supply ship arrived. With fresh provisions, the Astorians took on new life, but it didn't last long. Rumors of the war of 1812 reached the outpost, traders from the North West Company appeared. Aware of their predicament, threatened by the British presence to the north and conscious of the superiority of the British sea power, the Astorians, rather than have their fort captured, sold it to the Englishmen. Within a month, the British frigate *Raccoon* appeared. After sailing halfway around the world to do battle, all he had accomplished was to capture his own godforsaken fort!

The sudden sale and capture of Fort Astoria effectively destroyed Astor's plans for a Pacific trading enterprise. But Astor was not one to be easily discouraged. He concentrated on his Great Lakes territories and soon developed a virtual monopoly. Moreover, he expanded his activities in the West. And then, in 1834, when the American Fur Company was at its peak, John Jacob Astor retired.

In 1809 some prominent St. Louis businessmen organized the St. Louis–Missouri Fur Company. They sent a hundred and fifty of the best trappers, traders and hunters up the Missouri, establishing forts on the way. Their expedition, however, was fraught with troubles. At a fort on the Three Forks of the Missouri, Blackfeet Indians attacked and killed twenty-five men. Later a fire destroyed a large supply of their furs. Finally, the forts had to be abandoned. And yet, the St. Louis–Missouri Fur Company turned a profit.

As the years went by, fur companies came and went, merged and prospered. Small fortunes and great ones were made and sometimes lost. It was a business involving considerable financial risk and dramatic physical danger, including death. While the product was purely American, the market was almost entirely European, so was operated on a credit system. A span of approximately four years existed between the time the raw furs left the American traders' hands until the finished piece was sold and the credit, in the form of trade goods, finally reached the trader.

In the 1820s and 30s, the forts or trading posts on the Missouri were typical landmarks of the industry. They were, in fact, the heartbeat of the business. Fort Benton at the mouth of the Big Horn was established by the Missouri Fur Company as early as 1821, principally to attract trade with the Blackfeet and Assiniboine. Fort Laramie on the North Platte was erected by the partners Sublette and Campbell in 1834. Two years later they were bought out by the American Fur Company. Fort Pierre, built at the confluence of the Missouri and the Bad River, was situated, like Laramie, in the territory of the Sioux. It, too, was controlled by the American Fur Company.

The trading posts were managed by a *bourgeois*. He was responsible for ordering all the goods and supplies, fixing the prices, hiring the trappers and overseeing the trade with the Indians. In short, he supervised all the business. More often than not he was a partner in the company. The fact that the master of the post was referred to as the *bourgeois* is understandable, for the great majority of the men in the fur trade were Frenchmen. It was they who had pioneered the business in the first place, it was they who knew the wilderness like an Indian.

Second in command was the *partisan*. He was in charge of all field operations including the supervision of the rendezvous when no trading post was near. To keep records, a clerk was employed. In the absence of the *bourgeois*, he assumed charge. Often, too, he was a stockholder in the business. Other employees included a cook, a blacksmith, a carpenter and the "pork eaters." These men, under the direction of the "camp keeper," skinned the carcasses, dressed the furs, prepared the bales and performed sundry other choice jobs such as mucking out the horse stalls.

The key men in the fur trade, however, were the white trappers and the Indians. The trappers fell into two categories: company men and free trappers. The company men employed by the post generally left for the wilderness in the late fall to spend the winter in search of beaver. This was lonely work, for most men trapped on their own, setting their traps at remote beaver ponds. The man's equipment included traps, a rifle, shot and powder, a hunting knife and a hatchet. His most prized possession was his horse. More often than not he took to himself an Indian woman to mind his camp and keep him warm. The hazards of the work were very real. Blizzards and bitter cold, accidents, attacks by grizzly bears were dangers enough, let alone the constant fear of an Indian assault. As a consequence, the trapper's most valued equipment was a barrelfull of raw courage. And for all his skills, his hard work, his risks for a winter's catch of furs, the company paid him a salary of about four hundred dollars a year.

The free or independent trappers lived in much the same circumstances as did the company men, except that they gambled. They took the chance that they could trap more beaver and sell the pelts at a better price than the company men. They often shopped from post to post. Sometimes they did better and sometimes they did not. They bought their own equipment, supplies, sometimes even beads and trinkets to trade with the Indians on their own. All of this was done on

Left Indians examining a gun at a Hudson's Bay Company trading post
Above *Trappers' Rendezvous* by Alfred Jacob Miller. A welcome diversion in an otherwise lonely life
Below *The Trappers' Return* by George Caleb Bingham. A trappers life was a hard one and it is little wonder that many a trail was opened by these hardy pioneers as they moved westward

credit. The arrangement usually worked out very well, but not to the advantage of the free trapper. What with the trading posts discounting the value of the raw furs and jacking up the prices of blankets, tobacco, ammunition, sundry supplies and especially the price of rotgut whiskey, the free trapper was anything but free. By autumn, the time to set out on his annual expedition, the trapper was usually in debt up to his beard. The system worked neatly for the trading posts. They could be pretty certain that the not-so-free trappers would be back in the spring to trade.

If the company men and the free trappers were important to the fur companies, the Indians were essential. The pattern had been set in the last half of the seventeenth century. Trading for furs in exchange for blankets and copper pots, guns and mirrors, beads and whiskey was an established commerce. Intercourse with the Indian tribes, the Iroquois and Hurons, the Ottawa and Illinois and Miami was fostered and encouraged by the French, the English and later the Americans. The Indians were the hunters *par excellence*. They could bring in great quantities of furs, buffalo, deer, elk and smaller game, too. These supplemented the beaver pelts which the white trappers secured, for the Indians preferred not to trap.

While the great bulk of trading was carried out at the

posts, a pattern of rendezvous was also developed. This was true of the mountainous regions of western Wyoming and eastern Utah, an area where there were no forts. Here, once a year, traders bringing caravans of goods from the East would meet with free trappers and Indians from various nations. In one great and colorful binge of bartering, competing in games and contests of skill, they would drown themselves in drink. The merriment might go on for several weeks, go on until the last pelt had been bartered for the last bead. Then the eastern traders, their pack mules and horses laden with furs, would head for St. Louis, and the Indians and trappers disperse again into the wilderness.

The character of the trapper and mountain man is typified in the life of James Bridger. Born in Virginia in 1804, he moved to St. Louis where he worked as a blacksmith. One day in 1822 he noticed an advertisement in the *Missouri Republican* for a hundred enterprising young men wanted to head up the Missouri River, there to be employed for one, two or three years. To Jim this sounded attractive and he promptly hired on, exchanging the heat of the forge for the heat of the trail.

The idea had originated with two men named William Ashley and Andrew Henry. Rather than tie up large sums of money in constructing trading posts with the attendant cost of manning them and paying the *engagés*, Ashley would bring free trappers to the wilderness, meeting them later at a predetermined rendezvous where he would pay them off for their catch. This he would do either in goods or in cash, paying about half the amount he would expect to receive in St. Louis. Ashley was gambling on the spirit of free enterprise. Judging by the number of men who answered the advertisement, the plan was manifestly workable. Not only did Jim Bridger respond to the opportunity, but other men who were later to become famous joined up. Thomas Fizpatrick, William Sublette, Hugh Glass and Louis Vasquez were just a few of them.

Jim Bridger's first claim to a niche in history was hardly to his credit. During one of Andrew Henry's expeditions to the Yellowstone, the brash and daring Hugh Glass was savagely gored by a grizzly. So serious were his wounds that he was left to die. Henry offered to pay two volunteers to guard the dying man, give him a decent burial or, in the event of his recovery, bring him along west. John Fitzgerald and Jim Bridger volunteered. After a while, thinking Glass dead or tiring of their vigil, Bridger and Fitzgerald abandoned the trapper. They were careful to take his rifle.

But Glass was not dead. Weakly he dragged himself to a nearby spring which, by good fortune, was surrounded by wild cherry and buffalo berry bushes. For over a week he recouped here and then with only his razor for weapon, he lurched in an easterly direction toward Fort Kiowa on the Missouri. Along the way he came upon the carcass of a young buffalo being devoured by wolves. Frightening them off by setting fire to the prairie grass, he gorged himself. Once revived, he plodded on again for some two hundred miles until finally, half-starved, he reached Fort Kiowa.

Glass's immediate aim was to find his faithless companions and he made straight for the Yellowstone and the Bighorn River where he heard Henry was building

Above *Caravan en Route* by Alfred Jacob Miller. The American Fur Company's caravan heads for the Green River rendezvous
Below *Indians Returning to Fort Berthold* by Rudolf Kurz

a fort. Jim Bridger was understandably dismayed on learning of the resurrected Glass's impending arrival, so he was more than somewhat relieved when Glass did appear and, to the amazement of everyone, forgave him.

By this time, Fitzgerald was gone. Relentlessly Glass pursued him, running him down at Fort Atkinson the Missouri and giving him a tongue lashing to the effect that from now on Fitzgerald must live with himself and his conscience. Glass also got his gun back. Ten years later, Glass was again on the Yellowstone. This time his luck ran out. He and two companions were caught by the Arikara Indians and scalped. Such was the fiber and the fate of many a mountain man.

Jim Bridger fared better. Nor were his character and reputation damaged by the Glass incident. In 1835, in partnership with Milton Sublette and Thomas Fitzpatrick, he bought Fort Laramie, soon thereafter to be absorbed by the American Fur Company. Two years later he led a large party to the rendezvous on the Popo Agie.

Bridger was a big man, some six feet tall, powerfully built with a bull neck and altogether astonishingly athletic and sinewy. Yet for all his respected recognition as a mountain man, he could neither read nor write. In later years he became a teller of tall tales. One of them concerned a river composed of ice on the surface and boiling water beneath, another told of a glass mountain strewn about with the corpses of animals and birds that had run into it headlong. There was a third one about a boiling geyser that shot a spout of water three hundred feet into the air, yet another of a petrified forest with petrified birds singing petrified songs.

Jim's favorite story was of the time he was leading a large party of men through the mountain. Suddenly they were surprised by great numbers of Indians. The whites began to flee, the Indians pursued. As the trappers' horses tired, the men dismounted and ran for the protection of a wooded canyon. But the Indians were relentless, finally killing all the whites save Jim. Trying to escape, he progressed deeper into the canyon, only to find his way blocked by a waterfall bounded by rocky cliffs a hundred feet high.

At this point Bridger would stop, close his eyes in deep reflection. His listeners, anxious to hear the outcome, would urge him with a "What happened, what happened?"

"Well," Jim would reply with a sigh, "well, they shot me and buried me by the falls."

Among the important family enterprises in the fur trade, the Chouteaus were phenominal. In 1763, the fourteen-year-old Auguste accompanied his stepfather Pierre Laclède from New Orleans to establish a fort on the Mississippi. In the years following, the two of them began building a post at the mouth of the Missouri, a site that was later to become the city of St. Louis.

In time, Jean Pierre Chouteau, René's younger brother, also came to St. Louis and entered the family business. He and René commenced trade with the Osage Indians, a monopoly they enjoyed for over thirty years. When finally they lost it, they simply moved their operations farther west to what is now Salina, Oklahoma. The Osage obligingly moved their villages west as well.

It was in 1809 that Jean accompanied a party up the Missouri, partly to oversee the safe return of the celebrated She-he-ke to his Mandan village. This headman had agreed to visit Washington at Lewis and Clark's behest. The hostile Arikaras, however, were not about to allow a chief of the enemy to pass north through their territory and they attacked the party in strength, eventually forcing the traders to retreat downstream. And it wasn't until two years later, with a military escort of a hundred and twenty men and two hundred trapper-traders, that the Arikara were cowed and She-he-ke finally got home.

It was during this expedition that Chouteau apparently worked out arrangements for a business deal with the inimitable and wily Manuel Lisa. Lisa, born in New Orleans, appeared early in St. Louis. Like the Chouteaus, he traded with the Osage. Learning of the discoveries of Lewis and Clark, Lisa led a party up the Missouri beyond the Arikara villages. It was near here that he caught up with Wilson Hunt, leader of Astor's overland party. And it was he who effectively discouraged Hunt from proceeding into the Blackfeet country of Montana, recommending instead that he cross country. Lisa wanted the territory for himself. And when Jean Chouteau was endeavoring to return the Mandan She-he-ke to his people, it was rumored that it was Lisa who turned the Arikara against him, thereby reserving the northern reaches of the Missouri watershed for his own plans. At any rate, Lisa reached

Left Manuel Lisa, the shrewd Missouri fur trader who was ambitious and thoroughly disliked by all his competitors
Top *The Trapper's Last Shot* by William Ranney. An occupational hazard of the fur-trading game
Above Kenneth MacKenzie was a factor at the American Fur Company's Fort Union on the Missouri. The engraving is by Karl Bodmer

the confluence of the Yellowstone and Bighorn rivers. With the gates now securely shut behind him and well guarded by the Arikara, he erected Fort Raymond, naming it in honor of his son.

Lisa had the reputation of being hated by his *engagés* and thoroughly disliked by his competitors so it is surprising that Chouteau should have agreed to a business deal with him. Nonetheless, together with others, they formed the Missouri Fur Company. Lisa was to be the leader of expeditions. His influence with the tribes of the upper Missouri was extraordinary, so much so that during the war of 1812 he successfully retained their allegiance to the United States.

When Lewis and Clark reached the Mandan villages on their return home, John Colter, a member of the party, requested a discharge. Manuel Lisa had offered him a job. The proposition was for Colter to act as guide for Lisa's planned post at the headwaters of the Missouri. Colter accepted, trading the chance to see civilization again for a life in the wilderness. After reaching the mouth of the Bighorn where Lisa built his Fort Raymond, Colter was sent on to the land of the Crow Indians. Traveling farther along on foot, he reached the Wind River Mountains and the Grand Teton Range. Returning, he was seriously wounded in a battle between the Crow and Blackfeet Indians.

While Colter survived this foray with a bad leg wound, he was later captured by the Blackfeet. This time he was

stripped and his partner riddled with arrows.

The Indians debated as to the manner of torture they would put him through before killing him and decided to make him run for his life. Giving him a head start, they pursued. When the leading Indian finally threw his lance, Colter grabbed it, turned on his pursuer and ran him through. With the other warriors in hot pursuit, it is said that Colter dived into a pond and hid in a beaver's lodge. After the Indians gave up the chase, Colter staggered naked to Lisa's fort. It took him seven days.

Among the renowned mountain men, none was more respected than little five-foot-four-inch Kit Carson. As an orphan, he worked as a saddler at the eastern terminus of the Santa Fe trail. At the seasoned age of seventeen he quit and ran away. A wagon train headed for Santa Fe offered him his escape. And when he got to Santa Fe, he continued on northward to the fabled town of Taos. The life of the hunter fascinated him so he took it up and became most proficient. He proved his mettle at the rendezvous of 1835 when a hulking drunken bully of a trapper named Shunar threatened to eat up any Yankee he could find. Carson, already with the reputation of being a wildcat, cheerfully challenged the thug. Kit Carson outdrew him, shot him in the hand and brought the browbeater not only down to size, but had him begging for his life. In later years Carson became an important scout and guide and ended his career in 1867 as commanding general of Fort Garland, Colorado.

Of all the fur traders, none was more daring and determined than Kenneth McKenzie. It was he who opened the first post among the dreaded Blackfeet. As factor for the American Fur Company's Fort Union, he was a taskmaster and an elegant one. Among other things, he enjoyed fine brandy, so much so that he set up a still. This bit of illegality, however, jeopardized the company and led to his ruin.

It was in 1834 that a small change in men's hats appeared in Europe. For more years than men could remember, hats had been made of beaver felt. Now there were dandies sporting hats made of silk. The style spread and as more and more men chose silk hats, fewer men bought felt. And it was this little whim, this tiny shift in fashion, that within six years was a key factor in bringing the fur trade to an utter and irretrievable collapse. Coincidentally, the companies, in their competitive struggle to stay in business, had by this date pretty well trapped out the beaver. Men whose only way of life was that of exploitation now found they had hit the bottom of the barrel. In their avarice, they had shortsightedly destroyed the very basis of their existence. The change in fashion from beaver to silk added a nasty insult to a fatal injury.

Far left Christopher ("Kit") Carson, unsurpassed as a mountain man, was later a commander in the Indian wars

Left Jim Bridger, the trapper and mountain man who became part-owner of Fort Laramie. In his latter years Jim became something of a folk hero and a spinner of yarns many of which could be taken with a large pinch of salt.

THE INDIANS

The Indian was a barrier to westward expansion and little understood by the early pioneers. Both peoples came from complex societies and both came to fear and distrust the other. Skirmishes and reprisals became war and eventually led to the subjugation of a once proud race.

Above *The Buffalo Dance* by Charles Wimar
Right *Osage Scalp Dance* by John Mix Stanley

OF ALL the hazards to western expansion, none stood out more ominously to the white man than did the Indians. At the time of the Europeans' first arrival it is estimated that about one million Indians occupied what is now the United States and Canada. Some two hundred tribes speaking five distinct languages and scores of dialects flourished from New England to Florida, from California to Alaska. The nations of Indians had many and varied customs and ways of life, which to the Europeans invariably seemed strange and downright savage. And because the white man's drive for expansion demanded the very land that was the Indians', conflict was inevitable.

The Indians of the eastern woodlands were agriculturists and it was the women who tilled the fields of corn beans, squash and tobacco. They set their villages along the rivers which served as their principal routes of travel. The chief occupation of the men was hunting and warfare to which they were incessantly devoted.

Far south in Florida lived the Calusa, the Timucua and the Apalachee. To their north were such tribes as the Creek, Cherokee and Shawnee, the Tuscarora and the Powhatans of Virginia. In the Southeast were powerful and highly sophisticated groups like the Choctaws, Chicasaws and Natchez. In what is now New Jersey and eastern Pennsylvania lived the Delaware or Leni Lenapi, while in New York State the Iroquois Confederacy held sway. New England was the home of many small tribes with such fascinating names as Narraganset, Wampanoag, Pequot, Massachuset, Penobscot and Mohican. The region of the Great Lakes was the realm of the Ottawa and Huron, the Erie and to their west the Potowatomi, Menonini, Sauk and Fox. Farther south dwelt the Kickapoo and Winnebago, the Miami and the Illinois. And it was these Indians whom the white man had to destroy if a national destiny was to be fulfilled.

The Cherokee living in the western reaches of North Carolina and parts of Tennessee were typical of the Indians of the Southeast. Worldly wise, they were a powerful and populous nation of some twenty thousand souls. Governed by a council of elders whose decisions were reached only in unanimity, the Cherokee were an orderly people. Ceremonies were held throughout the year at the time of planting and at harvest. The latter was the Cherokees' New Year. A few days later, at the new moon, the people brought offerings to the sacred fire at the council house. Then, at an appropriate time determined by the priest, the perpetual fire was rekindled. People swept out the old fires, bathed in the river and let their old clothes drift away. Putting on new attire, they relit the fires and a new year was begun fresh and clean—the people being thus simultaneously purged of any enmity among themselves.

The women of the Cherokee not only cultivated the fields and tended the crops, but prepared all the palatable things to eat. Grinding the dried corn in mortars hewn from logs with sturdy five-foot pestles, they made corn bread and wholesome hominy. They knew all the wild roots, vegetables and fruits, onion and artichokes, potatoes and persimmons. Strawberries and blackberries grew in abundance and the women, having gathered the profusion, prepared them in all manner of delicious ways. These good things combined with roast venison or tasty quail, boiled bear meat or baked fish wrapped in leaves, made life for the Cherokee a culinary delight.

In addition to these chores in field and at the cooking fire, the women tanned the hides and fashioned the clothing, moccasins and robes, skirts and leggings. But most important, most vital to the continuity of Cherokee culture, was the woman's role as mother. It was she who tended to the needs of infants, watched over the play of small children. It was she who mourned the death of a son lost perhaps in battle.

The man's role, on the other hand, was that of provider and protector. As a boy he learned the skills of hunting and war. More often than not his games were directed at perfecting these skills. Others, however, like the rough-and-tumble lacrosse, were on the whole played for the sheer sport of it.

Upon marriage, a young man moved to his wife's village. Here he worked to support not only his wife, but her unmarried sisters, her younger brothers, her mother. He became, in fact, a cog in his wife's family enterprise. Rather than man and wife setting up an independent, conjugal family, a man married into a broad consanguine family composed entirely of his wife's relatives.

This arrangement had certain undeniable advantages, especially for the children. In the event of divorce or the death of a parent, the children, all belonging to their mother's extended or matrilocal family, were never left without close-knit kin, always present and responsible for their care.

Hunting was a man's chief activity and deer was the major kill. Most hunting was done on an individual basis, but on occasion men joined forces to surround game. While hunting was essential to sustain life, it was warfare that was the raison d'être of a man's life. As was true for so many of the Indian tribes, it was through battle that a man gained status and recognition. Whether in retaliation for a family member lost in battle or in defense of his village against enemy attack, men were quick to find an excuse to gain prestige.

To the colonists, the Cherokee were not only a strange and sometimes dangerous people to deal with, but they also stood in the way of what the newcomers considered a necessary and justified use of the land. Then, too, the Cherokee had sided with the British in the war of 1776 and the new nation was little disposed to be sympathetic to the Indian's request to save their territories. Irrespective of treaty after treaty wherein the Cherokees ceded land, treaties which promised no white men would trespass beyond the agreed line, the white men did trespass. As more pioneers and, later, speculators breached the borders to set up their illegal squatters' rights, new treaties had to be negotiated. And the Cherokees, under the gun of Carolina governors, acquiesced. The white man's appetite was insatiable.

In the North, the woodlands that were to become New York State were the land of the Iroquois. These Indians

Above *Penn's Treaty with the Delawares* by Benjamin West. William Penn, founder of Pennsylvania, was one of the few white men to keep his agreement with the Indians—an example that was to be followed by few others

had come to the area from the South in the distant past and had driven a wedge between such tribes as the Delawares to the east and the Hurons, Eries and Ottawas to the northwest. These men formed a remarkable confederacy known as the Five Nations. Spurred by the visionary concept of one Hiawatha, the Seneca, Mohawk, Onondaga, Cayuga and Oneida formed a league both for defense and aggression. And it was handsomely successful. By the mid-eighteenth century the Iroquois had almost annihilated the Huron and were now overlords of the Delaware and the Eries. At the same time, they welcomed the Iroquois-speaking Tuscaroras from the South.

The Iroquois form of government was an extraordinarily efficient and cohesive matriarchy. These people divided themselves into various clans with names such as Wolf, Deer, and Bear. At the head of each was a clan mother, and her role was one of supreme authority. It was she who decided who should be eligible from among the men of her clan to serve as headman or sachem. And if she became displeased with his decisions or his performance, she had the power to displace him.

As was true in many Indians societies, the Iroquois women were highly influential. Descent was reckoned through the female line as was property. It was the women who owned the bark houses, the utensils and the fields. Moreover, it was the women who arranged the marriages. The practice was to choose an older matron for a young man, and for a young girl an older man. Such a system had great merit. The girl was mated with a man experienced in hunting, well able to provide for her, besides being already acknowledged as a warrior with status. On the other hand, a young man married to an older woman acquired a wife skilled in the arts of housekeeping, child rearing and farming. In addition to these virtues, she had usually accumulated much property. Rather than take the risk of a pair of young newlyweds floundering in the mysteries of sex and the complexities of home life, the Iroquois system insured that at least one partner was experienced in marriage.

Iroquois men were not only the hunters and warriors,

but some achieved recognition as shamans and councilmen. As sachems, the elders met in the "Longhouses," making decisions through unanimous vote on matters of war and peace. During the French and Indian wars, the Five Nations stood with the British, chiefly because they were still smarting from joint French and Indian attacks under the command of Samuel de Champlain. As such, they controlled the fur trade in the region to the benefit of the British. At the outbreak of the American Revolution, the councils met to determine which side they would join. Their close relations with the British had for long been fostered by the able diplomatic negotiations of Sir William Johnson and his son-in-law, Guy Johnson. The councils of the Five Nations—Six once the Tuscaroras were included—acted nonetheless independently. The Seneca, Onondaga, Cayuga and Mohawks stayed with the British, the Tuscaroras and Oneida sided with the Americans.

As allies of the British, the Iroquois, sometimes independently, sometimes in company with British commanders, wreaked savage slaughter on the New York and Pennsylvania frontiers. The attack on the Wyoming Valley was a tragic example of the horror of frontier warfare. Only after General Sullivan's campaign was Iroquois power completely destroyed.

Crushing the Iroquois, however, by no means overcame the Indian barrier to western expansion. In the region of the Great Lakes, referred to in the eighteenth century as the "Northwest," there were many tribes—the Miami and Illinois, the Sauk and Fox and Potawatomi to name but a few. And while these nations were delighted with the benefits of the fur trade which brought them everything from pretty glass beads to firearms, they were less than pleased at the encroachment of white settlers on their territories. The treaty of 1795 had established a line beyond which the white man was not to cross, but the Indians could see that the line was a fiction.

Black Hawk, the leader of the Sauk and Fox, was acutely aware of the danger of the pioneers' transgression. His were a prosperous people living along the western shores of Lake Michigan. The women, as the

Left *Sauk and Fox Indians* by Karl Bodmer. The lands of this once-mighty nation were signed away under military duress
Top left *Cornplanter*—a portrait of an Iroquois sachem or headman
Top right *Black Hawk* leader of the Sauk and Fox
Above *Spring Frog*—a Cherokee

farmers, tilled fields sometimes consisting of several hundred acres. The men were the hunters and warriors. And the Sauk and Fox were extremely warlike. Desirous of the fertile bottomlands owned by the neighboring Illinois, they forthrightly made war, drove the Illinois from their valleys and simply took over.

The land of the Sauk and Fox was rich. Not only was the soil fertile, producing an abundance of corn, beans and squash, but the forests themselves were alive with game—deer, rabbits, beaver and bear. In the early fall, the Sauk and Fox left their bark house villages and migrated to the prairies to the west. Here they hunted buffalo and elk, collecting for themselves a winter's store of hides and meat. And when the signs of winter appeared, when the leaves were blown off the trees and the first snowflakes whitened the pine boughs, the Indians returned to their village. Once home, they would rekindle the fires and sit out the winter telling folk tales snug in their lodges.

But life for these Indians was not long to remain so idyllic. As early as 1804, white commissioners appeared with the firm intention of purchasing Indian land. Armed with the threat of military destruction, the commissioners literally forced the Sauk and Fox to "touch the pen" to a most unconscionable treaty. At three cents an acre it was extremely good business from the Americans' viewpoint. But for the Sauk and Fox, as was true for tribe after tribe, their naïve acquiescence was a sorry fatality. The Indians had signed away their lands and with them their way of life.

Moved to country west of the Mississippi, Black Hawk refused to accept the terms of the treaty. Instead, he and his son tried to enlist the aid of other tribes in regaining their tribal lands. Pleading with the Cherokee and Creek, the Winnebago and Osage to halt the white man's trespassing, he returned to his homelands. But his allies, their courage having wilted, dwindled away,

Above *San-Tan-Ti Addressing the Peace Commission at Council Grove* by Herman Stieffel. The Chief of the Kiowas parleys with the government at Medicine Creek in 1867
Left *Indians Returning from War* by Peter Rindisbacher. A warrior brandishes a dead enemy's scalp believed to restore the spirit of a fallen comrade

and he was left alone with only a small band of loyal followers. When at last he sent emissaries offering peace, the American coldly murdered them. Enraged, Black Hawk attacked. After meeting with some success, he retreated to the North. Here he was cornered. His white flag of surrender was ignored. Instead, the Americans viciously slaughtered the members of his band, men, women and children. Black Hawk escaped, but not for long. Soon he was captured and held in prison. In 1833 he was finally released and returned to Iowa to which remnants of his sad people had been sent. With the end of the Black Hawk War, Indian resistance to white settlement east of the Mississippi was smashed forever.

West of the dense forest lands, west of the muddy Mississippi, lay the Great Plains. Along the Missouri

River and its tributaries lived many tribes. Some were small groups like the Oto, Kansa, Ponca and Omaha. Others, the Pawnee and Arikara, the Mandan and the Hidatsa, were large and strong. Some, like the tiny Missouri and the powerful Osage, lived a semiwoodland life, venturing only onto the open plains for an annual buffalo hunt. All were farmers and like the Osage tended their fields in the summer and after harvest went on a fall hunt. With the exception of the Osage and Missouri, who preferred bark-covered wigwams and longhouses, their villages vere an assemblage of large dome-shaped earth lodges protected by a stockade.

Most northerly of these Indians were the Mandan. At the time of Lewis and Clark's visit, they were settled in two villages high on the bluffs overlooking the wide Missouri near what is now Bismark, South Dakota. At that time, they numbered about twelve hundred people. Once they were much more numerous and did not fear their enemies, the Sioux. As they explained to Lewis and Clark, smallpox had decimated their tribe and now they lived in apprehension. That they were once powerful is evident from the fact that they formerly occupied nine villages with a population of possibly eight thousand souls.

Mandan government was carried out by a council of priests and elders. These were men who possessed the sacred bundles of the tribe. Headmen, one peace chief and one war chief, were appointed from among themselves. These men acquired their positions in a variety of ways, partly through inheritance and partly through their prowess in war. Generosity, the ability to arbitrate and the performance of various ceremonies were also prerequisites for their high offices.

To assure the well-being of the people and a plentiful supply of buffalo, the Mandan performed an annual ceremony which they called the *Okipa*. Men not only gained much prestige by undergoing the ordeal, but could communicate directly with the great spirit Wakonda, the Sun. In this ceremony of self-torture, the candidates permitted skewers to be placed through the chest muscles. Thongs were attached to the skewers and thrown over house beams. The candidates were then pulled up by the thongs and left suspended a few feet above the ground thronged with singing spectators.

The ceremony lasted several hours and ended for the participants when they finally tore themselves loose. The Mandan believed that by means of this personal sacrifice Wakonda would grant them the blessings they sought.

The Mandans divided themselves into two groups or moieties, the Lefts and the Rights. These moieties were unevenly subdivided into thirteen clans with such names as the Prairie Chicken and Speckled Eagle. One might not marry a member of his clan nor within his moiety. Clan membership, inherited from the mother's line, brought with it special rights and privileges, including care of the sacred bundles.

While the Mandans suffered no military defeat at the hands of the Americans, they were indirectly destroyed with equal effectiveness. The white man's smallpox struck them first in 1782 and again in 1837. This time a mere thirty-nine woeful survivors wandered around their empty village. The Mandans simply didn't present any barrier upon which the Americans could vent their wrath.

If the Mandans were unable to resist the westward push of the Americans, the Indians of the western

Left A dramatic painting by Karl Bodmer entitled *Indian Warfare*, showing a combined force of Assiniboin and Cree attacking a band of Blackfeet at Fort McKenzie
Below Karl Bodmer's *Mandan Indians* depicts two warriors in full ceremonial regalia
Bottom *Indians Traveling* by Seth Eastman. A nomadic way of life was customary for the Plains Indians

Plains surely were. To the south, the Kiowa and Comanche, and farther north the Sioux, Cheyenne and Arapaho exhibited all the indignation of a cornered grizzly bear. The Crow, Blackfeet and Assiniboine to the northwest were so remote that they did not suffer the droves of white men crossing Indian country. Only at first did the Blackfeet show resentment to the vanguard of white men, the fur traders, and that was short-lived.

Of all the Indians of the high Plains, the Sioux probably best typified the dramatic character of these nomadic tepee dwellers, these buffalo-hunting warriors on horseback. The Sioux commanded a territory which included the western half of what is now South Dakota, the southern half of North Dakota bordering the Missouri River, as well as parts of Nebraska and eastern Wyoming. It just happened to be situated in the heart of the northern buffalo range. And as a consequence, the Sioux were rich. They were also haughty and belligerent as Lewis and Clark, with some uneasiness, discovered.

They had not always enjoyed this position of preeminence. Formerly living in the Mille Lacs region of Minnesota in the 1680s, they were driven from their country by the gun-carrying Crees. Gradually migrating westward, the Sioux crossed the Missouri. By 1742 they were well established on the Plains and it was about then that a fortuitous set of circumstances developed. By now the Sioux were receiving a small supply of firearms from French traders along the Missouri. At the same time, they were acquiring their first horses from the West. It wasn't long before this combination of affairs proved to be an unimagined advantage. Armed and mounted warriors had the upper hand of eastern enemies who had not yet acquired the horse and a similar superiority over western foes who had not yet received guns. With this good fortune, the Sioux became invincible.

While Sioux men often hunted alone for small game and deer, they hunted with well-organized teamwork when a herd of buffalo was sighted. Police, appointed by the leaders, saw to it that no hunter should break ranks. If one did so, the officers were authorized to tear down his tepee. At a given signal the mounted hunters chased the fleeing herd. The men with the fastest horses inevitably had the best selection, a two-year-old cow being considered choice. Its meat was the most tender, its hide was favored for making the finest robes. The successful hunter could become a good provider, be generous to others in sharing his kill and thereby gain prestige. Inept hunters who were unable to make a kill were entitled to tie a knot in the tail of a fallen buffalo. When the rightful owner returned to claim his quarry, he was obliged to share a quarter with the "tail tier." By this act of charity, the less proficient were provided for while the benefactor's reputation was enhanced.

Warfare, however, was the brilliant path to success. For the Sioux it was carried out for conquest and defense, for horses and in retaliation. The Black Hills were especially desirable as the habitat of wild game. Knowing this, the Sioux as early as 1776 drove out the Kiowa and took the Hills for themselves. They called them their "meat pack." As late as 1873, informed that a large Pawnee buffalo hunt was encroaching on their territory along the Platte River, the Sioux attacked. They drove off the Pawnees, killing over two hundred of them—again men, women and children.

Horses were the basis of Plains Indian economy. The value of a thing was reckoned by the number of horses required for its purchase. Magically painted shields and sacred eagle-feather warbonnets, vital protective devices in battle, each cost two horses. A bride might be worth

Red Cloud

Above *Red Cloud*, the Sioux leader who forced the United States to dismantle their forts

from four to twenty animals depending on the status of her family. But a herd of horses could only be obtained by stealing, which meant stealing from the enemy. Consequently, small war parties were constantly leaving the village on horse-stealing missions. Sometimes only two or three horses were borne off, on occasion a hundred or more head might be captured. And then there were times when the men returned not only empty-handed, but with one or more of their comrades left on the battlefield, scalped and mutilated.

In such an event, it was incumbent upon some male relative of the fallen warrior to vindicate his death, which entailed bringing home an enemy scalp. The Indians believed that human hair continued to grow after death and hence was associated with the human spirit and life everlasting. An individual who had been scalped could not go to the "Land of Many Lodges" until his scalp had been replaced. To accomplish this, a war party was organized with the express purpose of collecting scalps. As opposed to horse-stealing forays which set out on foot and rode their prizes home, vengeance parties left home on horseback. In a dawn attack, they might surprise an unwary and defenseless enemy village, killing a straggler here or there, or entice the enemy warriors away from their camp only to ambush them. Any scalp brought home would be presented to the mother or a close female relative with the words, "Here is your son. Rejoice, for now he is as one. Now he may join his loved ones in the Land of Many Lodges. Sing and dance with this and be happy."

Rain in the Face

Above *Rain in the Face*, a prominent Sioux headsman who fought against Custer

Partly because of the need for horses and partly because of their beliefs concerning scalping, warfare for the Plains Indians became a vicious circle from which they could not extricate themselves. It became a way of life. Warriors were foremost in prestige. War records were kept and recounted on every possible occasion. Men with the ability to acquire the most horses were held in the greatest esteem.

Property for the Sioux was of less value in itself than as an important commodity in the building of status and was in fact accumulated chiefly for the purpose of sharing it with others. Many ceremonies were performed for the moral benefit of the sponsor after which he was expected to offer gifts to the spectators. At these "give-aways" prestige rose or fell in proportion to the number and value of the items distributed. Giving a horse to the poor was particularly meritorious. For the Sioux, as with many tribes, the accumulation of property for property's sake was unthinkable. Only in giving a thing away did it acquire value.

To the Sioux, the emigrants on the Oregon Trail offered a distinct threat. The covered wagons of the 1840s, trailing along the Platte and through South Pass bound for Oregon, skirted the Sioux's southern border. The United States Cavalry, garrisoned at Fort Laramie, was responsible for protecting the caravans against Indian attack. Few forays occurred and casualties on either side were small. However, when the government began building a series of forts on the Bozeman Trail—a route to the Montana mining towns of the 1860s—matters grew tense. Red Cloud, an Oglala Sioux leader, declared open war on the military. With the battle against the party commanded by William Fetterman in 1866, the Indians practically closed the trail. In the treaty of 1868, the United States promised the Sioux that the route would be abandoned and the forts torn down. Red Cloud was the only man ever to force the United States to capitulate.

The Sioux's triumph, however, was as short-lived as an Indian summer. The ostensible reasons given for the subsequent systematic decimation of the buffalo herds were that they were needed as food for railroad crews and as a source of robes for the eastern markets. But the real and unadmitted motive for doing away with the buffalo, condoned if not openly supported by the government, was simply to starve the Indians into surrender. And by 1875, this is exactly what had happened. Hungry and unable to sustain themselves, the Sioux dejectedly accepted existence on land reserved for them by the federal government. Here the Indians were on relief, wards of the nation. Even worse, they were now victims of grafting agents who got rich by short-changing them on already meager rations. So incensed were such leaders as Crazy Horse and Sitting Bull at seeing their people starve that rather than rot on the reservations, they went to hunt the vanishing buffalo. It was better to starve as free men than die like cooped-up chickens in a pen.

This, of course, directly contravened the government's plan. The Indians had to be returned and returned subdued. The Sioux were thought to be somewhat east of Wyoming's Big Horn Mountains. An uncoordinated three-pronged pincer movement was organized by which General George Crook was to attack from the south, Colonel John Gibbon under General Alfred Terry from the northwest and General George Custer from the northeast. Crook, however, was never informed of Terry's schedule.

On the morning of June 25, 1876,the Sioux, together

Above *Buffalo Hunt* by Charles Russell. The buffalo was the mainstay of the Plains Indians' economy. Soon the white man was to drive the buffalo westward and the hapless Indians were forced to follow suit

with some bands of Cheyenne and Arapaho, were in fact camped along the west bank of the Greasy Grass River, known to the whites as the Little Bighorn. It was a big camp stretching three miles along the river with tepees enough for maybe ten thousand Indians. Sometime around three o'clock, the people in the Sioux camp were surprised by a charge of cavalry from the south. Hastily the warriors mounted their ponies and rushed to meet their attackers. They not only met them, but drove them off. Pummeling the outnumbered troops and their commander, a frightened Major Marcus Reno, into a frantic retreat, they pushed them east across the Little Bighorn and up the banks to the bluffs. Here Reno dug in and more or less awaited his fate.

Meanwhile, at the north end of the encampment, the Indians saw mounted troops riding along the high ridge to the east of the river. Alarmed, the men gathered their weapons, donned their magic warbonnets and rounded up their horses. Five Cheyenne warriors were the first to cross the river to stave off the enemy. Soon more and more cavalry appeared, some two hundred of them under the leadership of "Long Hair" as the Indians called Custer. But by now the Sioux had gathered their forces. Surging up the ridge, they stopped Custer and his men in their very tracks. Custer fought valiantly but was so outnumbered—twenty to one—that he had no chance at all. It was a short fight. Indian testimony suggests it may not have lasted more than an hour. Custer lost all his men, Indian casualties have been variously estimated. Red Horse, a Sioux participant, reported 136 killed and 160 wounded.

To the United States, celebrating its centennial, Custer's defeat was a shattering blow to its ego. For Custer himself, it was the end of a brilliant military career and the death of a vainglorious ambition. As a Democrat, he had hopes of being the party's presidential candidate. A dramatic, single-handed victory over the Sioux would, Custer believed, have cinched what he coveted.

The strategy of Terry, Gibbon, Crook and Custer to box in the Sioux never materialized. Crook had been defeated at the Battle of the Rosebud eight days earlier by the same Sioux now camped on the Little Bighorn. Crook had turned tail and headed south for the safety of Goose Creek. Though Custer was totally unaware of Crook's absence from the field, he was not even counting on him. His orders were to join with Gibbon, though Terry gave him a certain freedom of action when approaching the enemy. Leaving the mouth of the Yellowstone on June 21, Custer began using his freedom by carrying out forced marches. He had decided to smoke out the Indians a good day or two before the time appointed for his meeting with Terry and Gibbon. Even though Custer's Crow Indian scouts had warned him of a very large enemy encampment, Custer either did not believe them or disregarded their advice. At any rate, he hurriedly led his men on. Splitting his command, he stupidly sent Captain Frederick Benteen with the ammunition on a blind sortie to the south, altogether away from where the Sioux camps had been sighted.

Geronimo

General George Custer

Custer also sent Reno to the west with the promise that he would be supported. For whatever reason, Custer failed in his promise. Instead, he rode north along the ridge and came in view of the Sioux camp on the west side of the Little Bighorn. From his vantage point he could plainly see Reno's engagement, but instead of helping, he and his aides merely waved their hats. On they rode northward. And rode right into a well-deserved catastrophe.

Custer and his men made history in about sixty minutes. The Sioux enjoyed a brilliant though short-lived victory. Unwittingly they also saved the United States the possibility of electing for its President a willful, headstrong and pompous disaster.

Defenders of Custer see him as a forceful, bold and daring commander who liked to kill Indians. It was a task in which he reveled, having proved himself earlier at the Washita by killing over a hundred Cheyenne in a surprise winter attack. In 1876, this was still considered by many a laudable thing to do. Detractors of Custer, however, see him as an arrogant, lustful braggart. It is revealing to note that while most of the troopers of his Seventh Cavalry were scalped and their bodies mutilated, Custer's remained untouched. There was good reason for this. The Sioux believed that a scalp represented the spirit of a man and that filling a fallen enemy's body with arrows and cutting off his fingers and genitals rendered his spirit harmless. No longer would he haunt the world of the living. They also believed that the scalp of the murderer, the homosexual and the suicide was of no value. These were people

Chief Joseph

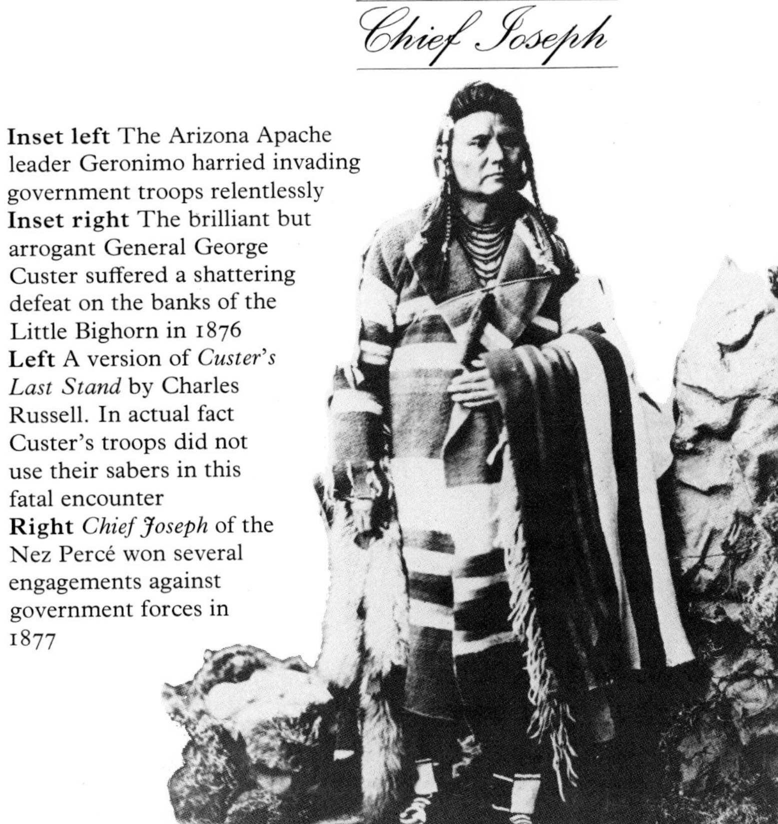

Inset left The Arizona Apache leader Geronimo harried invading government troops relentlessly
Inset right The brilliant but arrogant General George Custer suffered a shattering defeat on the banks of the Little Bighorn in 1876
Left A version of *Custer's Last Stand* by Charles Russell. In actual fact Custer's troops did not use their sabers in this fatal encounter
Right *Chief Joseph* of the Nez Percé won several engagements against government forces in 1877

who never entered the Land of Many Lodges but lived in a separate limbo, people to be shunned and outcast. Custer's body was found with a bullet hole in the chest and one in the forehead. Not a hair on his head had been touched.

Like the Sioux headmen, leaders of other tribes resisted the onslaught of the white men. Chief Joseph of the Nez Percé valiantly fought the government troops, Geronimo led his Apaches on constant attacks against the army. Both men, however, succumbed to the overwhelming strength of the invaders. It was not until the winter of 1896 that the Sioux were subjected to their final ignominy. Believing in the teachings of a Paiute seer, Wowoka, who taught that by performing certain ritualized songs and dances, the buffalo and the ancestors would return and somehow the white men would just disappear, the Sioux danced and sang. Alarmed by a congregation of Sioux practicing the "Ghost Dance," the United States cavalry confronted the Indians. A shot was fired. Fighting broke out. The Sioux men defended themselves with their meager weapons, the women with their bare hands. The cavalry

retaliated with fire from an automatic repeating cannon. Before it was over, 146 Indians were killed, 25 cavalrymen were dead. Here, at Wounded Knee, the seventh Cavalry had vindicated the loss of its former commander, George Armstrong Custer.

With the massacre at Wounded Knee, over two hundred years of genocide came to an end. The Indians would no longer be driven from their homelands or hunted to extermination. Safely isolated on their reservations, they no longer posed a threat to the white man's destiny.

Below *Song of the Talking Wires* by Henry Farney. The telegraph brought to an end the brief but heroic period of the pony express. Soon communication was to push ahead again in the form of the railroad and the "Iron Horses" that marked further inroads into what was formerly Indian Territory

THE OPPORTUNISTS

The drive West had begun in earnest and settlers started to organize themselves for the journey. Believing there to be safety in numbers they formed caravans and hired trappers as guides. Organization was prudent as the obstacles were great; the heat of the trail, the threat of winter for those whose progress was too slow and the ever-present danger of an Indian attack.

Above *Buffalo Hunt* by Charles Russell
Right Eager settlers in a race for homesteads

As early as the eighteenth century, colonists were making determined efforts to occupy land to the west, to carve out tiny farms, to establish small settlements in the fertile valleys of the unending forest lands. Moving from the coastal regions, they reached the foot of the Appalachian Mountains from the Carolinas north to Pennsylvania.

Englishmen and Germans and Orangemen from the north of Ireland, colloquially referred to as "Scotch Irish," were among the most intrepid of the pioneers. There were hard men who had little to lose. For the most part they were independent to the point of blatancy. While it is true that they relied upon the eastern cities for such commodities as copper pots, knives and axes, firearms, powder and lead for making balls, and maybe a book or two, they were amazingly self-sufficient. Their chief crops were corn, wheat, rye and oats, surpluses of which they shipped East. Most of the men supplemented their agricultural labors with hunting. The meat they fed their families, the hides they used to make clothing or sold for cash. They were famous for their marksmanship, and it was the invention of the rifled barrel that made the Kentucky rifle so superior a weapon.

One of the most resolute of frontiersmen was Daniel Boone. A Pennsylvanian by birth, he and his family moved South to a little valley in North Carolina called Yadkin. He never made much of a record as a farmer, but kept his wife and children somewhat supplied with meat from his continual hunting trips. The buckskins he brought home could be converted into cash. Worth a dollar a hide, the term "buck" has long been part of the American vernacular. But Boone was hunting for more than game. The policy of the colonial governments was one whereby East Coast investors were permitted to speculate in large tracts of western land. They could get rich selling acreage to potential settlers. Many of the frontiersmen, however, having already staked out holdings for themselves in advance of the land grants, hoped to hold their claims by a sort of squatter's right. They gambled on being able to pay for a proper title when the time came.

The squatters reasoned that since they had cleared the land and tilled the fields, they were putting the land to use. Thereby they had a prior right. The speculators argued differently. In most cases the eastern interests prevailed. The settlers forfeited their shaky claims, picked up their belongings and again moved farther west.

Daniel Boone, aware of this problem, marked out likely farmlands on his hunting trips, marked them out by blazing the trees. But he did more than that. He cozied up to Judge Richard Henderson, a westerner of questionable ethics, who speculated in land. Henderson financed Boone to make a survey of the West. And what

Left *Daniel Boone Escorting Settlers Through the Cumberland Gap* by George Caleb Bingham. Such a trek was fraught with hazards, including Indian ambushes

Boone saw impressed him deeply. Here was an abundance of wildlife, salt licks and lush valleys. And while working for Henderson, Boone marked out desirable tracts for himself, feeling assured that what he had selected would be honored by the judge.

When Boone returned, his tales whetted the appetites of the settlers. Already angered by the attitude of the governor who, safe in his palace at New Bern, favored the eastern financial interests at their expense, they were quick to follow Boone to his newfound paradise.

Boone became something of a hero. It was in 1773 that he led his first party of anxious settlers across the mountains to the beautiful valleys of Kentucky. The beautiful valleys, however, belonged to the Cherokee Indians and the treaty of 1763 had specified a boundary beyond which no white man might pass. If Boone failed to recognize the line, the Indians didn't. They promptly drove Daniel and his followers off, killing Boone's eldest son in the skirmish.

Squire Boone was not one to give up easily. Back where he belonged, he urged Judge Henderson to lay claim to the western lands before someone else did. And Henderson acted. He formed the Transylvania Company, raised ten thousand dollars' worth of trinkets, traded goods and firearms and forthwith made a treaty with the Cherokee. Without any trouble at all, he bought the better part of Kentucky and Tennessee. While it was absolutely illegal for an individual to treat with the Indians for land, this didn't seem to bother Henderson. He immediately set Boone to carving out a trail through the mountains, the Wilderness Road as it came to be called, a rough and rugged highway to Transylvania. When the original trail was completed, Boone established a small fort near what is now Lexington, Kentucky. He named it Boonesboro. It was in March, 1775, that Boone, like a conquering hero, led his people to the land of hope. They were buying the land of course, from Henderson.

Once the settlers got to Transylvania, they wouldn't pay for the land. Henderson was losing his shirt. It came to him that North Carolina and Virginia might bail him out. Adding a county to one of the colonies for an agreed sum would certainly help defray expenses. But the governors were furious at his high-handedness and would not recognize his claim. Henderson tried another tack. The colonies were just now proclaiming their independence at Philadelphia. Henderson sent an emissary to the newly formed Continental Congress with the proposition that Transylvania be incorporated as another state. He really had little to offer save some wilderness and a dream. The new Congress, like most following Congresses, fumbled for months and then at last made a definite decision by tabling the whole matter. The upshot was that Henderson lost all claim to Transylvania. Only years later was he granted a measly tract of land in compensation for his expenditures. The exquisite little valley was insignificant and moreover was miles and miles beyond the farthest reaches of western settlements. Judge Henderson, scoundrel that he was, had been had.

Daniel Boone, whose only worth was his buckskin shirt, never lost it. He was made of different stuff from Henderson. His was the true spirit of itchy feet, euphemistically termed *wanderlust*. A little man standing only five feet six inches, he was well and powerfully built. Blue-eyed and black-haired, he was regarded by some as good-looking. As was customary with most frontiersmen, he wore Indian buckskins and often a coonskin cap. While illiterate, at best barely able to write his name, he was bold and wise in the ways of the Indians and the forests. During one of his forays in search of salt, he was captured by the Shawnee. Instead of being put to torture and killed, he was adopted into the tribe, though kept well under guard. In 1778 he was taken by the Indians to the British-held fort of Detroit. Here he pleaded the British cause and they offered to buy him for a hundred dollars, but the Shawnee, who regarded him highly, refused to sell and took him back with them. Despite the Indians' precautions, he eventually made his escape. After an incredible four day trip through the wilderness sustained by only one meal, he returned safely to Boonesboro. Once there, he warned the residents of an impending attack, a raid which thanks to his foresight ultimately failed.

Always moving westward, he founded Boone's Station, Kentucky, then Maysville where he set up a tavern. Though his land holdings were extensive, most of his claims were found to be defective. He lost them all in land suits. Angered, he moved to the Spanish territory of Louisiana and in 1799 was granted a large tract of land. With the Louisiana Purchase, his title was again found to be worthless. Only through the intervention of Congress was some of it restored. Living with his sons, he saved money enough to pay off his debts. But the urge to move was still strong in him. In 1814, at the age of eighty, he made a hunting trip to the Yellowstone River. Upon his return, he felt hemmed in by the growing numbers of settlers and planned yet another move. Death, however, intervened. He died in September of 1820, having lived eighty-six remarkable years.

The pioneer spirit exhibited by men like Daniel Boone, the need for elbow room, the hope for a better life in greener pastures lured Americans West in greater and greater numbers. Indian borders were continually being pushed back as well as being violated. By 1830 the line of settlement approximated the Mississippi River. And it was about this time that Hall J. Kelly, a Boston schoolteacher, had a dream he could not dispel. Depressed by the loss of Fort Astoria to the English, yet inspired by the potentialities of Oregon, he read and studied everything he could lay his hands on about the territory. So enthusiastic did he become that he gave talks and wrote articles about the wonders of Oregon. Yet Kelly had never been West. By 1833 he had so convinced himself and a few reluctant others of the wonderful prospects in Oregon that he led a small party as far as New Orleans. Here the loyal followers threw in the sponge. The inconveniences of the trip were surpassed only by Kelly's bumbling and the immigrants went home. Kelly was determined. He made his way alone from Vera Cruz across Mexico, where the Mexicans promptly confiscated his property and supplies. To recoup his losses, Kelly rounded up some cattle with the plan of driving them to Vancouver in the hope of selling them to John McLoughlin of the Hudson's Bay. But McLoughlin, renowned for his hospitality, took Kelly for a cattle thief and treated him rather shabbily. On top of this, Kelly contracted malaria and almost died. Finally, hard-luck Kelly was put on a ship and eventually arrived back in Boston again in 1836. His dream had become his nightmare.

Kelly's dream, however, became reality for others. Not only was colonization being promoted, but Christianizing the Indians was also a popular goal. As early as 1835, Marcus Whitman and Samuel Park spent some time in the Green River region proselytizing the heathens. Convinced that more and more money was needed to do an effective job in bringing the true religion to the Indians, Whitman decided to go back East for help. There he gathered more funds from the Presbyterians and Congregationalists. He also gathered himself a wife, a Narcissa Prentis. She proved as inspired a missionary as her groom. In the spring of 1836, Whitman and his bride, together with another newly married couple named Spaulding, headed West on what turned out to be one of the longest honeymoons on record.

The men provided wagons so their brides might ride, but after reaching what is now Boise, Idaho, the conditions were so bad that the women had to walk. Upon arriving in Oregon, the Whitmans set up a mission among the Cayuse Indians. Here, surrounded by a few scattered colonists, they not only administered to the Indians' ills, but extolled the advantages of the Christian faith. Things went well for several years, until a plague broke out among the natives which Whitman could not cure and the Indians accused the

Above Judge Richard Henderson, land speculator, made an illegal treaty with the Cherokee and lost his shirt
Right Hall J. Kelly's dream of a paradise in Oregon turned to nightmare

good missionary of starting it. He had been observed giving a patient medicine from a bottle. The Indians concluded that the contents contained the source of the epidemic and forthwith destroyed the mission and killed Whitman and his wife.

Despite Whitman's sad demise, tales of the wonders of Oregon continued to infiltrate the eastern mind. It was John Frémont's expedition of 1843, however, that dramatized the marvels of Oregon and the possibilities of practical settlement. Frémont had already commanded an exploring party to the Rocky Mountains in 1842, his guide being the inimitable Kit Carson. This latest Oregon trip, again led by Carson, took them through Nevada, across the Sierras and into California. It was Frémont's lengthy, detailed and glowing report of the region that gave the real impetus to the great migration that followed. Congress came alert and ordered that a hundred thousand copies of it be printed. Everyone wanted to read about the dashing "Pathfinder" as Frémont was dubbed, as well as the wonders he described.

Men like Fremont were not the only ones to describe the glories of the West. George Catlin, a Pennsylvania lawyer turned artist, had an inspired idea. This was the

period when taxonomy was the stylish scientific approach and Catlin set for himself a monumental project. As Audubon was painting all the birds of North America, so Catlin would paint all the Indians.

As early as 1829, Catlin was painting Iroquois Indians and the next year he was as far west as Fort Leavenworth making portraits of such transplanted eastern Indians as Shawnee, Delaware, Potuwatomi and Kickapoo. In 1832 he was able to reach Fort Union on the steamboat *Yellowstone*. On this trip he painted portraits of the Sioux at Fort Pierre, Crow and Blackfeet at Fort Union. He also spent several days at the Mandan villages painting various village and ceremonial scenes, including his famous portrait of the chief, Four Bears.

Left An unknown artist's impression of John Frémont, the "Pathfinder", whose glowing reports sparked off the migration to the West
Below *Fort Vancouver* by Captain James Warre. British control of the Pacific centered on this Hudson's Bay Company post
Right George Catlins's *Four Bears* shows the Mandan chieftain wearing a shirt decorated with the symbols of his exploits which emphasized his power and prowess

The following year Catlin accompanied a troop of dragoons on an expedition to the southern Plains where he sketched members of the Kiowa, Comanche and Wichita tribes.

By now Catlin's ambition to make a definitive collection of paintings depicting Indian life was becoming a reality. The first showing of his Indian Gallery was held in Pittsburgh in 1833. New York gave his paintings a gala show in 1837. Now he was acclaimed. Later, exhibitions were held in other eastern cities, culminating in a London show which drew crowds for five years. His crowning glory was an invitational showing at the Louvre for King Louis Philippe.

Along with his ability as a painter, he wrote copiously. His *Letters and Notes on the Manners, Customs and Conditions of the North American Indians* was a landmark bringing to the public heretofore unknown information about the native Americans. Catlin's works were not only a monument to the man himself, but an invaluable ethnographic and historical contribution to the world.

Karl Bodmer, a young Swiss artist, was of a different temperament from Catlin. A highly skilled draftsman, he had no ambition whatsoever to create an Indian gallery. But he did. Commissioned to accompany scientifically minded Maximilian, Prince Wied-Neuwied, on an expedition of North America, Bodmer was the official artist. Leaving St. Louis in the spring of 1833, they traveled up the Missouri on the *Yellowstone* heading for Fort Union. While the prince made field notes and collected specimens of plants, animals and Indian paraphernalia, Bodmer made detailed watercolor sketches. So superbly accurate were his paintings of the flora and fauna and of Indian life that they are unsurpassed both in ethnographic fidelity and dramatic portrayal of the western scene.

The young artist and the prince, his mentor, spent a little over a year on the upper Missouri. Then they returned to Europe where Bodmer spent the following year refining his pictures and supervising the production of hand-colored lithographs. The prince began collating his own material. Finally, in 1839, Maximilian published the spectacularly authoritative *Reise in das Innere Nord-America in den Jahren 1832 bis 1834* filled with handsome plates of Bodmer's wonderful Indians.

Captain William Drummond Stewart, a veteran of Waterloo, was bored stiff with his life as second son of a Scotch nobleman. The gloom of Murthly Castle palled on him, unrelieved by the fact that his elder brother would inherit the family fortune while he at best would be left with a pittance. To counter these doldrums, Stewart spent his time game hunting here and there about Europe. Intrigued by word that then reached him of distant Louisiana, he decided this rugged, untouched land was the ideal challenge to his *ennui*. And with this as spur, off he set, to become the West's first and most colorful sportsman.

Arriving in New York in the spring of 1832, he made his way to St. Louis by canal boat and from here by riverboat to New Orleans. A year later, guided by the fur trader Robert Campbell, he was on his way up the Mississippi River heading for the West. His destination was the fur-trading rendezvous where Horse Creek flows into the Green River in what is now Wyoming. Here in this dazzling wilderness of rushing streams and grand mountains, Stewart was enthralled. The hunting was fabulous and so were the people. To him the Indians were proudly free, unspoiled creatures of nature, while the trappers were true heroes of the mountain vastness.

Stewart was quick to make friends with such stalwarts as Jim Bridger and Antoine Clement, and with Bridger left the rendezvous for an extended hunting trip as far north as the Big Horn Mountains and as far south as Taos, New Mexico. Vancouver was included as well and it was not until November, 1835, that Stewart returned to New Orleans.

While there, he happened upon the paintings of an artist named Alfred Jacob Miller. Stewart so liked his style that he suggested that Miller accompany him on his next trip. Miller was young and jumped at the idea. He didn't care what he painted, he just wanted to paint. It was in the spring of 1837 that Stewart started out. Miller made dozens of watercolors along the way and was having a great time. He made pictures of Fort Laramie and the Sioux, of the mountain men and the great rendezvous on the Green. And his impressionistic renderings were much to the captain's taste.

After the rendezvous of 1838 at the Popo Agie, Stewart learned of the death of his brother. Even though he was now Sir William, he did not rush to claim his castle. First he gathered up his collection which included two live buffalo, a grizzly bear, two young Indians and the trapper Antoine Clement. Then with this menagerie Stewart went back to Scotland.

Right Alfred Jacob Miller's impression of Sir William Drummond Stewart and Antoine Clement

The buffalo wandered around the estate while Clement donned a kilt and tried his hand at waiting at table. Miller worked on in New Orleans polishing his paintings for his patron. In 1839 he had an exhibition in New York which was much praised. Later he became a virtual artist-in-residence at Murthly Castle and eventually settled in Baltimore as a successful portrait painter. Except for his New York show, Miller's work of the West lay pretty well hidden in Scotland and in the private collection of a patron, William Walters, and the Peal Museum in Baltimore. Unlike Catlin's and Bodmer's pictures which received wide recognition through publication, Miller's endeavors saw little light until a century after their execution.

The migration to Oregon began on a small scale in 1838, spearheaded by Thomas Jefferson Farnham. In 1842, a hundred and thirty pioneers set out under the leadership of Elijah White. It took eighteen wagons to haul their belongings. Marcus Whitman had shortly afterwards led a thousand immigrants West. And between the years 1845 and 1847 from three to five thousand opportunists hit the trail for Oregon.

Most of the caravans were assembled at such towns as Independence, St. Joseph, or Westport, now Kansas City, along the Missouri River. The majority of pioneers were Missouri and Iowa farmers. Disgruntled at the poor prices they had received for the crops following the depression of 1837, and feeling generally hemmed in, they decided to make a new start in the Promised Land. Saddled with all their worldly possessions, pots and pans, guns and ammunition, chairs and tables, beds and bureaus, even cows and chickens, they now bought supplies for the trek. Flour and sugar, beans and bacon were the staples. They might also buy a wagon, and mules and oxen to pull it. A few of the wagons were

Below *The Rocky Mountains, Emigrants Crossing the Plains*—a colorful print evoking the romantic appeal of the West
Right *Conestoga Wagon* by Thomas Birch. A "Prairie Schooner" heads westward. These wagons had to carry a family and their entire possessions and rightly earned their place in the history of the West

Conestogas, those sturdily built "Prairie Schooners" designed for the rough roads of the East, many more were box wagons fitted with high, curved ribs over which canvas was stretched to form a cover. Protection against both the searing sunrays and the drenching rains was essential. The hope was that, what with all their belongings there would be space enough inside for at least the women and children to sleep and find privacy.

It was planned that the caravans should leave as soon as the grass was tall enough to provide forage for the livestock. When the party was ready, a guide was employed, invariably a retired trapper and mountain man who knew the route. In addition, a member of the party was elected as captain or wagon master, if frequently not until several days after the wagon train had departed by which time everyone would be better acquainted and able to make a sounder choice.

The day began punctually at dawn with the sounding of a bugle. After breakfast, the mules and oxen were hitched up and by seven the procession was on its way. Shortly before noon the wagons were halted for the animals to graze and the people to prepare a midday meal. Not until about three in the afternoon did the caravan start up again. The women and children rode in the wagons, if there was room. The men and boys, walking alongside, or riding a horse, had the job of herding the livestock. At dusk the wagon train stopped for the night and was drawn up in a circle, the tongue of each wagon being pushed under the rear of the next as a defense against Indian attack. The livestock were often corralled inside as an additional precaution.

Left The American dream: not all who set out on the 2000-mile trek along the Oregon Trail to California struck it rich

Below A group of determined-looking homesteaders in the Loup Valley, Nebraska

Well-organized caravans had a definite route and schedule. About fifteen miles a day was what they needed to cover if they were to reach the Cascades before the October snows. Trying to cross the mountains in winter would be sheer disaster. Leaving the Missouri, the route cut northwest over the rolling prairies of eastern Kansas until it reached Fort Kearney on the Platte. From there it followed the river past Chimney Rock and the impressive stone ridges known as Council Bluffs. About forty-five days after leaving the Missouri, the pioneers should have reached Fort Laramie, a welcome resting place. The men repaired the wagons, fitting new iron tyres when necessary, shoed the oxen, mules and horses. The women washed the clothes. This was the last stop where they could refit and obtain supplies.

From Fort Laramie the trail led northwest, still along the Platte, past Independence Rock, the granite landmark on which many carved their initials and the date as mementoes of their progress. At the confluence of the Sweetwater the trail headed due west through the gentle South Pass at the foot of the Wind River Mountains. By now they had been fifty to fifty-five days on the trail nearly nine hundred and fifty miles from their starting point. And it was about now that tensions mounted, quarrels exploded and dissension led to ugly brawls. Blame for conditions was generally directed at the wagon master. More often than not he was displaced by someone else whom the group felt had stronger qualities. It was here that laggards were often left behind to fend for themselves, or gave up and more wisely turned around for home. Following tributaries of the Green River and then the Green itself, the course

dropped in a southwesterly direction to Fort Bridger. From there it turned north along the Bear River to Fort Hall in Idaho.

Now their real troubles began. Following the Snake River west toward Fort Boise and on toward the Whitman Mission in Oregon was barren country with good water in scarce supply. High-growing sage clogged the wagons. River crossings were as difficult as they were hazardous. The draft animals were worn and tired. To relieve the strain, dispensable luxuries such as stoves and bureaus were cast out to litter the trail.

It was a troublesome trip over the Blue Mountains and down the Columbia from the mouth of the Umatilla River. Here the Oregon Trail officially ended and the wagons had to be abandoned. All the goods and belongings were stacked on rafts or sometimes in canoes for the trip down the Columbia. A few foolhardy souls lashed their wagons to a raft and in some cases were lucky. More often the raft capsized with its top-heavy load and everything was lost including a few pioneers.

Altogether the trip to Fort Vancouver and the ocean was over two thousand miles from Independence, an ordeal which took about five months.

To those for whom California was the goal, the route split at the Snake River west of Fort Hall, with the travelers dropping south along the Raft River and past the strange natural formations called the City of Rocks. Progressing farther, they would reach the Humboldt. Here the going was made easier by an abundance of grass and good water, but traveling westward through the Humboldt Sink was a nightmare. Marshy with saltwater bogs, progress was slow and precarious. Beyond the sink lay an arid desert backed by the almost impenetrable Sierra Nevada Mountains. The Truckee, a turbulent, boulder-strewn river, led up to Donner Pass, and from there the trail led down to the California valleys of the Sacramento and San Joaquin.

While the Oregon and California trails were the principal routes west, others were tried, if generally given up as too difficult. The hardship endured on

these trips was often acute. Not only did the livestock die for want of good grazing and water, but sickness and death overtook many of the pioneers themselves. Cholera was especially feared. Tragedy appeared in the form of broken bones, drownings and small children falling out of wagons to be crushed under the wheels. Danger of Indian attack was ever present, though the very numbers of wagons and people served as a deterrent to the warriors. Actually very few engagements occurred. Short cuts were sometimes plotted which might save many miles, but were often so hazardous as to be barely worth the time saved. An example was the Sublette cutoff on the Oregon Trail—fifty miles without a drop of water from the Green River west to the Bear.

Small, independent parties were subject to the most danger. Often they were composed of a few determined individuals who believed they could make it without benefit of scout or guide. The Donner party was one. Emigrants from Iowa and Illinois, the Donner and Reed families, to save time since they were running late, foolishly decided to take a short cut. Known as the Hasting's cutoff, it ran from Fort Bridger south around the Great Salt Lake. It turned out to be a hellish ordeal over endless salt flats. Arguments flared over the wisdom of Reed's choice of the route. He was bombastic, but knew nothing of the terrain. Donner was old and knew

less. When they reached what is now Donner Lake, high in the Sierras, they stopped to recoup their strength. By now it was mid-October and resting at this time was disastrous. Suddenly a great blizzard engulfed them. Short of supplies and fuel, they tried to dig in, building little cabins to ward off the wintry gales. By December, one group of seventeen could stand it no longer. Risking the deep snows, they tried to make it down the mountain enduring untold suffering during their trek. It took them over thirty days before they reached the lowlands. The trip had cost them the lives of six men and a boy, each of whom they ate. Meanwhile, the sixty or so members who remained behind were slowly starving. Those who did not die from want of food were freezing to death. Frantic from the pangs of hunger, they began to devour their dead companions. By the time they were finally rescued, there were barely thirty survivors.

The Mormon migration to the West had its origins in central New York State in the 1820s and started with a family named Smith. Old Crooked Neck Smith suffered fits from time to time. His grandson Joseph, like other members of the family, delved into the occult. Joseph

Below *Attack on the Emigrant Trail* by Wimar. The ever present danger of an Indian attack ended the trek West for many settlers

also wore a little stone in his hat which he claimed enabled him to find gold hidden in the earth.

It was in 1827 that, according to his own account, Joseph's mystical vision revealed to him the whereabouts of some fabulous golden tablets. Although Joseph was close to being illiterate, he translated the inscriptions by means, so it is recorded, of a pair of magic glasses, and was astonished to learn that the tablets contained certain missing books of the Bible. The translation became known as the *Book of the Mormon* and referred to the lost tribes of Israel, two of which, amazingly had found their way to America. One was the good Nephites, the other the cruel Lamanites. The Lamanites, who were reputedly the Indians, totally annihilated the Nephites, all except one named Mormon. His sacred mission, as Smith interpreted these revelations, was to conquer the Lamanites.

Smith published the book, but at $1.75 a copy, a price revealed by God, it didn't sell very well; so God reduced the price to $1.25. Soon enough people had studied this newfound gospel for Smith to believe he had sufficient followers to form the Church of Jesus Christ of Latter-Day Saints. It wasn't long, however, before neighbors began to ridicule the Saints so much that in 1831 the converts moved to Kirtland, Ohio. Here Smith organized a communal colony from where he sent out missionaries. So successful was their proselytizing that a thousand new converts were recruited. Among the missionaries was a recent convert, Brigham Young.

Smith, besides being spiritual leader of the Church, was also the banker. As such, he amassed considerable wealth in land and small industry. In his divine capacity, he received revelations which banned such earthly pleasures as smoking and the use of alcohol. Somehow, the revelation concerning abstinence excluded Smith. He drank and smoked as he pleased.

Again the neighbors mocked the Saints. Apprehensive of the strength of their communal economy, skeptical of their being true Christians, hearing rumors that they indulged in polygamy, the good people of Ohio showed their distaste by giving Smith a good tar-and-feathering. With that hint, Smith promptly received a revelation that Independence, Missouri, was the new Promised Land.

At Independence, the Mormons built a temple, worked hard and prospered. But here again they antagonized their gentile neighbors. Pitched battles erupted and finally the Mormons once more pulled up stakes. Offered a haven in Illinois at a town they named Nauvoo, they began life again. Their industry was phenomenal. By 1840 Nauvoo was one of the larger communities in Illinois, numbering ten thousand people and growing daily.

Smith was a willful man. He demanded complete autonomy for his Mormon "state"—his own courts, his own militia, his own monetary system. In 1843 Smith announced a new revelation that sanctioned polygamy, whereupon he took to himself twelve wives, a situation his first wife, Emma, was enjoined to accept without complaint. Not long after this, Smith had the gall to run

Above A consciously posed work gang, with relatives, on the framework of a barn. Co-operation was the key to survival on the frontier

On the Mormon Tr

Brigham Young

Joseph Smith

Above The settlers faced additional terrors from natural causes, as illustrated in William Ranney's *Prairie Fire*
Right *Westward Ho* by William R. Leigh shows emigrants fighting off an Indian attack

for the presidency of the United States. But this only increased already existent animosities. By 1844 Smith and his brother Hyrum had so angered the surrounding communities that they were arrested and charged with treason. Imprisoned in Carthage, Illinois, though not very securely, they were murdered by a mob that stormed the jail.

With Smith's death, the Saints were now left without a leader. There were several candidates vying to fill the vacancy, but it was Brigham Young, largely responsible for maintaining a measure of unity in the wake of the assassination, who was finally elected to succeed Smith. In a very short time Young proved himself to be an able and strong leader, one who was more concerned with sound organization than with pomposity.

The ill feelings aroused by Smith, however, did not disappear with his death. Rather, they seemed to swell, finally reaching the point of active religious persecution. Matters grew so tense that Young decided there was no choice but to abandon Nauvoo. Again the Saints left their homes, their shops, their industries and their beloved temple. Almost aimlessly they moved westward, with no fixed destination in mind.

Young was familiar, however, with Fremont's journals. It occurred to him from descriptions he had read of the Great Basin and Salt Lake that this might be a region remote enough for the Mormons to carry on their way of life unmolested. And so the decision was made.

Boldly setting out across the Plains, their spirits were sustained by a little brass marching band. At night the

sawing of fiddles broke the monotony. When the advance party had eventually worked its way through South Pass, they happened upon Jim Bridger. Young learned from him more about the Great Basin and that the land east of Salt Lake might be habitable. The party continued on, dropping south from Fort Bridger toward Salt Lake. Finally, after a most toilsome trip, someone spied the great shining body of water. Cheers went up and the party took on revived life. The Mormons were amazingly quick to choose a site for their new home. They had to be. It was now the end of July, 1847. Crops needed to be planted if the people were to survive the winter. The earth was sunbaked to the hardness of brick, but they diverted a stream, plowed the moistened soil and hurriedly planted corn, beans and potatoes.

Mormons continued to arrive at Salt Lake City. One group, lacking wagons and draft animals, pushed and pulled handcarts over the long trail. The next year Young led nearly three thousand Saints to their new home. No sooner had they arrived than disaster threatened. A plague of grasshoppers descended over the fields, menacing all the crops. Starvation would be imminent. And then, almost as though from nowhere, a great flock of gulls appeared. In what was claimed as a beneficent act of God, the birds devoured the insects and the crops were saved. With this divine blessing, the Mormons went on to lay out streets and build a new temple. They also erected a statue to the gulls.

Whatever the prejudices people may have held against them for their beliefs and way of life, no one has ever had anything but the deepest respect for the Mormons' fortitude, frugality and industry.

Not all trails west were trod by pioneers and the Santa Fe Trail was one. It was begun exclusively for trade with Mexican settlements in and about Santa Fe. Until the Mexican Revolution in 1821, the Spanish Southwest was effectively sealed against the Americans. But with the lifting of restrictions, a lively commerce soon began. Freighters generally collected their wares at Independence, Missouri, and loaded them into Conestoga or sturdy Pittsburgh wagons. These were drawn by as many as twelve oxen or mules. Mirrors, woolen shawls, yard goods of silk and cotton, tools and hardware accounted for the bulk of the three to five thousand pounds of merchandise that made up the cargo.

From Independence, the freighters headed west, each leaving separately in the spring as soon as ready. At Council Grove, Kansas, they waited for one another until all had assembled, enough to form a great caravan. From here on the danger of Indian attack, especially by the Kiowas and Comanches, was constant. Strength in numbers was an essential consideration. Here the trip was organized, captains chosen, night guards assigned to duty, cooks selected. Nothing was left to chance.

From Council Grove the trail led southwest to the

Big Bend of the Arkansas and on along that river for some hundred and twenty miles. There the trail split. The main route continued along the river to Bent's Fort and then south to Santa Fe. The short cut dropped southwest in a direct line to the old Spanish capital. The short cut was quicker, but was fraught with a nasty hazard, the Cimarron Desert. Most traders chose the desert route.

In Santa Fe the traders sold their goods. They sold over a million and three-quarter dollars' worth in 1846. Some of this money was spent on mules and horses, pelts and bars of gold. These they took back with them on the return trip and sold at a handsome profit. The Santa Fe Trail, for those who dared risk it, yielded no mean jackpot.

The colonizing of Texas differed from that in most other regions in that the contenders there were not Indians but the Spanish. As early as 1800, a certain Philip Nolan decided to make some money by capturing wild horses west of the Brazos River. Instead, he was attacked by Spanish troops and killed. Zebulon Pike was commissioned in 1806 to explore parts of Texas, but since this was Spanish territory, his mission was more in the nature of a spying one. The Spaniards captured him, although he was later released. In 1820, however, a Yankee from Connecticut named Moses Austin, in the hope of recouping his finances, was bold enough to propose to the Spaniards a grandiose scheme of colonization. The Spanish agreed, but Austin didn't live long enough to see his plan fulfilled as he died on the way home.

Above *Emigrants Attacked by Indians* by John S. Davies. By the time they reached their journey's end both women and children knew how to load a gun
Below One of the hazards of the Santa Fe Trail depicted by Seth Eastman in *Emigrants Attacked by Comanches*

Austin's son, however, inherited his father's enthusiasm. He completed the transaction with dispatch and by 1822 had enlisted a hundred and fifty settlers. Each man was to receive 640 acres, his wife 320, and each child 60. For this they were to pay the awesome sum of twelve and a half cents an acre.

The Mexican Revolution of 1821 scared Austin and he rushed to Mexico City to validate his rights. Not only did he secure them, but he was granted 354 acres of farming land and 66,000 grazing acres on the understanding that he would bring two hundred families enticed by the prospect of acquiring 177 acres for farming or 4,428 acres for grazing. Austin was successful in his recruiting. The American settlers were for the most part from Kentucky and Tennessee, shrewd Germans and Irishmen. They were quick to take the four-thousand-acre grazing grants. By 1827 it was estimated that there were ten thousand Americans in Texas and by 1835 there were over three times that many.

As time passed, the Mexican government began imposing restrictions upon the colonists—custom fees, military posts and the closing of the borders to further American immigration. The Americans, as might be expected, resented any curtailment of their imagined freedoms. Talk of Texas as an independent nation or as a territory of the United States spread as bickering with Mexican authorities increased. It was during this period of tension that Sam Houston, a lawyer and former congressman, as well as a former governor of Tennessee, wandered on to the scene. As a politician, he thought he knew a good thing when he saw it. It was in 1830 that he first advocated that the best interests of Texas lay in becoming part of the United States. He even wrote President Andrew Jackson to that effect, suggesting that Jackson take over.

The Mexican Revolution of 1821 was won in large measure by the generalship and personality of Santa

Anna. Nor is it surprising that he shortly after assumed for himself the role of dictator. At first he took a benevolently liberal approach to the governing of Texas. At least Stephen Austin thought so. He went so far as to urge his fellow Texans to remain loyal to Mexico and to work harmoniously with it for a smoothly running country. But Santa Anna's liberalism was, as is true of all military dictators, as fake as sugar frosting on a poisoned cake.

The Texans did not take kindly to Santa Anna's plans for them. Santa Anna, on the other hand, took even less kindly to rumblings of a revolution. Backed by six thousand troops, he was fully intent on and thoroughly capable of quashing it. It was in October, 1835, that the Texans hastily met in convention to prepare for the dictator's invasion. They elected Henry

Smith as provisional head of the government and Sam Houston as military commander. While the title sounded impressive, Houston didn't have much to command. His forces were divided as well as dispersed. W. B. Travis had a hundred and fifty men at San Antonio, Grant and Johnson at St. Patricia commanded a hundred, Fannin was at Goliad with four hundred, while Houston had three hundred and fifty men at Gonzales.

Above *Wagon Box Fight* by O.C. Seltzer. This standoff was fought in the summer of 1867

At word of the Mexican advance, the Texans under Travis determined to defend San Antonio. Having already destroyed the hundred men at St. Patricia, Santa Anna attacked. Outnumbered, the Texans were forced to retire to a small fortified chapel called the Alamo, resolved to hold it against the army at all costs.

Left Sam Houston's victory at the Alamo assured the independence of Texas
Below Santa Anna captures the fort of the Alamo, leaving no survivors. It was this action that was to be his undoing as the whole of Texas rallied to the cry of "Remember the Alamo". One month later the Mexicans were put to flight and Santa Anna was captured

While there were only one hundred and eighty-four men, they were daring, independent and superior marksmen. Among them were such renowned frontiersmen as James Bowie and Davy Crockett.

Santa Anna was confident in his superiority and demanded surrender. Travis refused and on February 24, 1836, the siege began. For over a week the defenders held out against hopeless odds. Not until March 6, in a bitter hand-to-hand struggle within the very walls, did Santa Anna take the fort. Not a single Texan was left alive.

While Santa Anna enjoyed a resounding military victory, the fall of the Alamo gave the Texans a moral one. Everywhere the settlers rallied to the cry, "Remember the Alamo." Volunteers joined Houston in increasing numbers until soon he had some fifteen hundred recruits under his command. Because of the Mexicans' greater numbers, however, Houston was compelled to take delaying actions. Not until April did the armies meet. It was at San Jacinto Ferry that Santa Anna, cocksure of his strength, relaxed his vigil. This was his mistake. On the afternoon of April 21, the Texans charged. Inspired by the cry, "Remember the Alamo," they completely surprised the Mexicans. The encounter was brief, and while shots were exchanged, the Mexicans soon broke ranks and fled. The next day Santa Anna himself was captured. The victory was complete and Texas was no longer under the Mexican yoke.

The increasing number of pioneers, freighters and, later, miners and railroad builders were under perpetual threat of Indian attack. To the Kiowas and Comanches, the freighters on the Santa Fe Trail posed not only the danger of further inroads into their own territories, but were also on occasion a plum to be picked. It was not until 1829, however, that protection in the form of a military escort was provided. Unfortunately, the infantrymen trudging along beside the wagons were only partially effective as guards. Better protection was needed for the rich cargoes and the "mule skinners", or wagoners, who drove the teams. By 1833 ten companies of dragoons were assigned for the sole purpose of patrolling the Southwest. Under Colonel Stephen Kearny, they rode around the southern Plains with a show of arms intended to intimidate the Indians. Not much happened, but at least there were no fights.

To the north along the Platte River, the Oregon Trail ran through the southern territories of the Sioux. While at first the Indians allowed the wagon trains to pass unmolested, the immigrants were nonetheless in constant fear. To afford them protection, mounted troops were garrisoned at Fort Laramie. Recently purchased by the government, from the American Fur Company, it served as a base for later forts along the Bozeman Trail leading to the Montana mining towns.

The first real trouble with the Sioux came as the result of a worn-out cow. It was mid-August, 1854, and a group of immigrating Mormons were approaching Fort Laramie. As they passed near some Sioux villages a few miles east of the fort, a footsore cow somehow escaped the caravan. Before its owner could catch it, a young Miniconjou warrior playfully shot at it and butchered it on the spot. When the Mormons reached Fort Laramie, the owner reported his loss to the commandant, Lieutenant Hugh Fleming, in the hope of restitution. Fleming didn't give the matter much attention. Even when Conquering Bear, chief of the Brulé Sioux, with whom the Miniconjous were camped, came to the fort to try to settle the matter, Fleming was pretty casual. The chief even offered to try to persuade the young warrior to turn himself over to the military, but nothing was settled.

Among the officers under Fleming's command was a brash shavetail lieutenant named James Gratten. The next day he was able to convince his superior that with a force of twenty-nine men and two howitzers he could easily take captive the Miniconjou culprit and bring him back to justice. Fleming naïvely agreed.

Gratten knew nothing about Indians. Foolhardily, he marched his troop straight toward the Sioux villages where close to five thousand Indians were camped. It is estimated that there were over a thousand fighting men—Oglalas, Brulés and Miniconjous. Past the Oglala camps and on to the Brulé he went. Confronting Conquering Bear, he demanded the Miniconjou. The chief could not produce him. Instead, he offered two of his horses. Gratten grew impatient. Suddenly he quit conferring and willfully commanded his men to shoot toward the Indians. Conquering Bear ordered his warriors to hold their fire, but when Gratten had the cannons fired, the Indians could no longer be restrained. In a matter of minutes, swarms of angered Sioux warriors surrounded the troops, wiping them out to all but one man. Conquering Bear was mortally wounded, Gratten was the first to be killed.

The sole surviving trooper escaped to hide in a nearby trading post, but died of his wounds two days later. And so, with the loss of one dumb cow, the Sioux wars began, not to end for over thirty-five years.

The life of the trooper was a combination of absolute boredom when confined to the forts and of great danger requiring courage and endurance when on campaigns. All sorts of men joined up. Victims of hard times and economic depressions, immigrants from Europe, especially Germans, Irishmen and Italians. Debtors and petty criminals with a choice of enlisting or serving a jail sentence happily volunteered. Restless young boys tired of the monotony of farming enlisted with the enthusiasm of kids going to a circus. The pay was enticing—$13 a month for enlisted men, $117.50 for officers. With good army food, comfortable lodgings and a clothing allowance, the risk of an arrow in the back seemed well worth taking.

Actually, throughout all the Indian wars, most battles were short and casualties were small. This fact, of course, was little consolation to the victims, either Indian or soldier. Nonetheless, the government funneled vast sums of money to the Army, partly to insure the safety of the travelers, more importantly to effect the complete subjugation of the Indians. Some student of arithmetic calculated that it cost the nation a million dollars for every Indian killed. The price of manifest destiny was not necessarily cheap.

Many were the battles—the Fetterman and Wagon Box, the Sand Creek, Beecher Island and Rosebud, to name but a few. Some were decisive victories for the Army, such as Custer's surprise massacre of the Cheyenne at the Washita. Many more were standoffs and a few were utter disasters. In this last category, Custer capped the record.

And so the West was won. By 1850 it had been thoroughly explored and to a degree exploited. The fur trade had pretty well destroyed the beaver population while gold miners were just beginning to scratch the surface in their lust for the precious metal. The country east of the Mississippi was already filled and farmers as far west as Iowa were feeling cramped. California and Oregon were now the meccas. While it would be another quarter of a century before the Indians would be subdued or the railroads and telegraph would tie the nation together, the pattern of manifest destiny was firmly set. Nothing could stop this crusade of national expansion, for the Americans felt increasingly challenged by this chance to conquer the difficult. Hard work, frugality and faith in God were the keys to economic security, social recognition and quite possibly safe passage through the Pearly Gates. And with that spirit, the Americans made the hard seem easy and the impossible merely hard.

THE COWBOYS

Cattle trails gave rise to cattle towns with unforgettable names like Abilene and Dodge City. This was the era of the range wars, the result of great rivalry between cattlemen and nesters. These troubled times produced men like Billy the Kid and John Wesley Hardin. It was a rough world in which outlaw and lawman recognized that the most effective kind of law was the six-gun.

Below *The Fall of the Cowboy* by Frederic Remington
Right Cowboys around a chuck wagon

IT IS STRANGE that the real hero of the West turned out to be not the indomitable explorer, the hardy trapper, the colorful Plains Indian in warbonnet and paint, nor even the pioneer girded with fortitude, but rather the lonesome cowboy.

It all began in Texas. After the Civil War, Texas was an economic shambles. Returning veterans found their herds of livestock scattered, lost here and there all over the mesquite wastes. It was to the cowboys, who rounded up these animals, drove the herds on their long northward treks, that Texas owed as much as to anyone the start of its new-found postwar prosperity.

The cows the Texans owned, if they could find them, were offshoots and strays of Andulusian cattle that the Spanish introduced to the New World. For the *hidalgos* operating their huge *ranchos* from their *haciendas* in the Southwest, the cattle were valuable for their beef, hides and tallow. Wiry Indian *vaqueros* were employed to tend the stock. But the region was vast and even the most vigilant herdsman had little chance of checking all the wayward, ranging cattle. Many animals just wandered off, soon to be lost in the barren desolation that was Texas. As the years went by, these wild strays developed several rather astounding characteristics. In addition to their tremendous size and their ability to forage as many as fifteen miles from water, they possessed a huge set of horns sometimes measuring seven feet from tip to tip. And it was these Longhorns that formed the basis of the early cattle industry.

The idea of bringing cattle to northern urban centers in the hope of finding a market was not new. As early as 1855, some cowboys drove a herd as far as New York City. As they kept no records, little is known of the result of the drive other than that they didn't try it again. But as the railroads pushed farther west, so the burgeoning eastern population clamored for more foodstuffs. Now cattle would be driven north to railhead towns in Kansas to be shipped East. And drive their cattle north the Texans did.

Several trails led north and some, like the Shawnee, the Chisum and later the Western, became famed. A typical cattle drive required considerable planning and even more hard work. First the cows had to be gathered and it took a persisent cowboy and a rugged horse to flush the critters from the dense thickets and deep gulches. When at last enough cattle had been rounded up, they were sorted according to their brands. Next a count was made so that each owner had a record of the steers belonging to him. Unbranded animals, referred to as "mavericks," were frequently divided up among the owners since there was no possible way of telling to whom they belonged. It was not uncommon for cowboys to spend their free time rounding up mavericks and marking them with their own brand. Many a Texas herd was begun in just this way.

On occasion the cattlemen might join forces and make the drive, but more often they would sell their cattle to a professional drover. Ike Pryor, an experienced trail driver, expected to pay about eight dollars a head. At the end of the trail he would sell the cattle for perhaps twenty dollars and make a killing. He calculated his expenses would include a dollar a day each for nine cowboys, a hundred dollars a month for a "trail boss" or "ramrod," fifty dollars for the cook or "Old Lady" plus all he could eat. Besides needing sixty to sixty-six horses, he would have to buy provisions costing about three hundred dollars. Pryor figured a herd of a thousand head would pay off. Costing a dollar a head per mile,

Trail Drive by W.H.D. Koerner. Men, horses and Longhorns all needed tremendous stamina

less expenses, loss of cattle through death, strays and theft, he might well enjoy a profit of thirty thousand dollars. But if stampedes, drought, a blizzard or a shrunken market at the railhead should befall him, a drover could easily lose just about everything.

The most experienced cowboys or "point drivers" led the herd. Along the main body rode the "line riders," while at the rear, pushing the lazy cows amid a cloud of dust, were the "greenhorns." About their only equipment was a loud "halloo" and a mustang for a cow pony. The cook's chief supplies were bacon and beans, flour, coffee and a shovel. He was generally hired for his ability to drive a team of horses, his culinary accomplishments being invariably a matter of secondary concern.

The average drive began by pushing the "beeves," a term used for any animal over four years of age, at a pretty good clip. Experience had taught that by driving the cattle hard for twenty-five or thirty miles, some say even more, and tiring them out, there was less chance of the "coasters" bolting for home. The first few days of the drive were difficult. Cattle continued to try to turn back, obstreperous young steers seemed bent on fomenting a stampede just for fun. Cowboys were quick to spot these recalcitrants. They either cut them from the herd and turned them back or simply shot them. Green beef was much better than rancid bacon.

The experienced drover knew where the waterholes could be found, where to bed the cattle down for the night. At dusk, the drive was stopped. The horses were "cavvied" in a "remuda," an improvised rope corral, while the cook prepared the evening meal. The cowboys were sent on night watch, usually in two-hour shifts, their job to ride around the herd comforting the cows with little songs.

Cowboy songs were many and important and a wrangler who couldn't sing just might not get hired for the job. A stampede was frighteningly dangerous, a disaster which as often as not meant not only loss of cattle, but injury and death to the men. Cattle were extremely nervous. A bolt of lightning was almost certain to set them off in a mad rush, but even the mere striking of a match might spark a stampede. And about the only prevention the cowboys had were their doleful little songs.

When a stampede did break loose, every cowhand was called into action, every one but the Old Lady. The hope was that by riding to the head of the herd, it might be turned in on itself. By circling and thereby milling, the steers might exhaust themselves and finally come to rest. Some cattle were known to have run over forty miles before coming to a halt, another bunch stampeded eighteen times in one night alone.

It often required several days to round up all the cattle. And there were also times when the men had to search for a fallen companion, trampled to death by a myriad of sharp hooves. It was then that the Old Lady brought out his shovel. The remaining cowboys would stand briefly around the shallow grave, their hats in hand and that was about it.

A drover hoped to average about fifteen miles a day with luck. It was a day that started at dawn with a hot breakfast of bacon and coffee, beans and soda sinkers. A noon meal of about the same fare gave time for the men to rest and the cattle to graze. Even though cows were bought and sold by the head, not by weight, they sold more readily and for a better price if they looked on the fat side rather than like a gaunt and walking mass of bones.

CMRussell

This series of paintings shows the grasp of detail that Charles Russell possessed. These three episodes illustrate the brief incidents that were a daily part of a cowboy's life and which demanded a quick eye for trouble and some pretty deft horsemanship.

Left *Dangerous Moment* **Above** *Bronco Busting*
Below *The Broken Rope*

At best the Longhorn was not the ideal beef animal. Despite its great size, it was slow to mature and slow to fatten. The tremendous horns were a distinct liability, for when the animals were crowded in cattle cars, the stilettolike points punctured and bruised both hide and muscle. But they were hardy, they could thrive on the barest of "pickings," forage for miles and go without water for over forty-eight hours. And it was these attributes that made them ideally suited to the long drives to which they were subjected.

The cow pony was an equally robust beast. A combination of wild mustang escaped from Spanish herds of the seventeenth and eighteenth century and horses the Texans later brought from Kentucky and Tennessee, he was quick, so close-coupled he could turn on a cow chip and possessed of an endurance and stamina that could withstand a tornado.

There were many rivers to cross from southern Texas to the railroad towns of Kansas—the Colorado and Brazos and Red to the south, the Canadian, the Cimarron and the Arkansas to the north. "A mile wide and an inch deep" was no misrepresentation, but when spring rains came these rivers were transformed into raging torrents. Every river had to be forded, there was not a bridge across a single one of them. When the herd reached a river, the point riders usually plunged their horses ahead while the herd was pushed hard in hopes of keeping up the momentum. One old drover, Colonel Snyder, had two old swimming steers who rushed in first to lead the cattle on. Too often the animals became nervous either at the swift currents or at snags and floating logs. If the herd began to mill or even turn back, the cowboys had to swim their horses among the cattle trying to force them forward. Should a cowpuncher be thrown from his mount, he might grab its tail or try to make shore by swimming. Not a few men lost their lives by drowning. Yet whatever the trouble, there is no record of a herd ever failing to cross a river.

While dust choked the cowboys most of the time, rain drenched them. The only protection was their yellow oilskin slickers and their wide-brimmed hats. No tents were carried on the drives so when the men weren't peacefully sleeping under starry skies, they were wallowing around in rivulets and mud. But then when a man was making a dollar a day, a few little inconveniences could be happily put up with.

As if stampedes and swollen rivers were not eough, after the drovers crossed the Canadian River, they faced man-made obstacles. The country north of the river was Indian Territory, later to become Oklahoma. Here lived members of the Cherokee and Choctaw, Chicasaw and Creek tribes. Highly sophisticated, they were successful farmers who were incensed at having the herds of Longhorns trample their crops. Being resourceful, they retaliated. Appearing in large numbers armed with menacing weapons, they demanded a toll. Sometimes the fee was a given number of steers, sometimes it was ten cents a head, sometimes both. The cowboys had no choice but to ante up.

If the Indian Territory was bad, Kansas was worse. The Yankee farmers, calling themselves Grangers, resented the Texas cattle grazing across their lands as much as did the Indians. Moreover, they were frightened into meanness for fear their own cattle would contract the dread southern tick fever, a disease to which the Longhorn was immune. Like the Indians, the angry Grangers also appeared as armed vigilantes, barring passage to the railhead. Nor were some of the honest Kansans above serving as middlemen for cattle buyers in the railroad towns. Before they would let a herd pass, they saw to it they got their cut.

To make matters still worse, drovers were plagued by marauding bands of outlaws known as Jayhawkers. These rowdy villains brazenly demanded tribute. If it was not forthcoming, they simply shot up the cowboys and stole the cattle. The cowboys themselves were not bad shots and more than one Jayhawker was left unburied on the prairie, prey to the blowflies and the buzzards.

All this was very tough on the Texans. Stuck below the Kansas border, grazing land wore out, the cattle grew thin and the drover was losing money. When at last the herds were pushed through to such railroad towns as Abilene, Ellsworth or Dodge City, great and boisterous was the celebration.

Not all cowboys knuckled under to the Kansans. Nelson Story was one who didn't. Rather than allow his herd of a thousand head to stay bottled up south of Baxter Springs, he decided on a daring move. Story had been a freighter on the Oregon Trail, had struck it rich in the gold mines of Montana and knew there were ten thousand meat-starved miners in the vicinity of Virginia City. Besides, his bride lived there.

First, Story evaded the Kansas border guard simply by moving his cattle west. Then he circled his herd north to Fort Leavenworth where he outfitted a wagon train. With bullwhackers, oxcarts and new Remington breech-loading rifles, he was ready for anything. Along with twenty-seven men he drove his herd west over the Oregon Trail to Fort Laramie. The Bozeman Trail ran north toward Montana, and while it was protected by a chain of forts, it was alive with hostile Indians. This didn't bother Story one iota. Onward he pushed. Near Fort Reno, Sioux warriors attacked, drove off several cows and wounded two of Story's men with arrows. Story didn't hesitate. He and his men pursued the Indians, shot them up with his new Remingtons and retrieved every last cow.

When Story and his herd reached Fort Kearny, he found one very frightened commander, Colonel Henry Carrington, in charge. The colonel refused Story passage, the trail beyond being too dangerous. Instead, he ordered corrals to be built to hold the cattle. Since Carrington reserved the grass close to the fort for his horses, the corrals, while in sight of the post, were too far distant for adequate protection.

Story chafed under his confinement just so long. And then he took matters into his own hands. In a vote he took of his men, all but one elected to push the herd on against Carrington's orders. Immediately the man who had voted to stay was trussed up and bundled into an oxcart. And then, under cover of darkness, Story moved the cattle out.

Now they drove the cows by night and let them graze by day. After a day on the trail, the man who had wanted to remain behind was given his freedom to return to the front. This time he emphatically decided to remain with the party. Some days later a scout, several miles ahead of the herd, was found dead on the trail, scalped and pinned to the earth with arrows. Story was unable to rescue him. Twice more the Sioux attacked and both times were repulsed by the hot fire of the new Remingtons. Finally, on November 9, 1866, the herd trailed into Virginia City to a gala welcome, made even more so for Story by the sight of his wife riding out to meet him in a wagon.

While men like Story bypassed the Kansas cow towns, most drovers worried it out with the Grangers, Jayhawkers and speculators and finally got their cattle through. But tensions increased and hatred mounted to the extent that it became all but impossible for buyers and sellers to do business. And then a man named Joseph McCoy had a brainstorm.

McCoy was a cattle dealer from Illinois aware of the entire problem. He was also alert to the fact that railroads were gradually laying their tracks of steel ever farther west. After a good deal of cajolery, he was able to convince the leery directors of the Kansas Pacific Railroad that a westerly line to the little town of Abilene, Kanas, would be profitable. The town fathers were elated and became enthusiastic supporters, especially when McCoy agreed to put up considerable money.

The idea was that McCoy would build a hotel together with great holding pens. Here at Abilene, well west of the settlements, cowboys could drive their herds straight to the railhead unmolested. No longer would they be held up at the Kansas border. McCoy would take a modest commission on each head sold and that would suffice as his recompense. McCoy sent an agent south to the Texas drovers who happily and with astonishing speed turned their herds westward. It was a great scheme and everyone was overjoyed. Abilene became a boom town almost overnight. It took a little longer for McCoy to go bust.

As the railroads pushed west, other cow towns sprang up, the most westerly of which was Dodge City. The drovers carved out trails leading to them—the Chisum led to Abilene and Ellsworth, the Western later to Dodge. Reaching the towns was a time of jubilation. After nearly a thousand weary miles the cowboys had truly reached the end of the trail. Here the drover cashed in for all his gamble and his work and paid off the cowboys. With money in their pockets, maybe as much as a hundred dollars, they hit the town. Roaring up and

Above The Dodge City Cowboy Band. They supplied their own percussion!

down the streets, they went from bar to gambling house to brothel and then back again in a wild celebrating spree. To these men who had passed through the gates of hell, Abilene, Ellsworth and Dodge City were heaven.

The cow towns were really studies in iniquity. The men who operated the flashy saloons and gambling houses, the madams who took charge of the glittering houses of ill repute were at least forthright in making capital from wickedness. The businessmen, while delighted at making a fast buck, hypocritically tried to look the other way. But matters got so bad, what with the drunken brawling and blatant whoring, with knifings, shootings and killings, men dying of lead poisoning in the streets, that the townsfolk finally took action. Hiring a sheriff who was quick on the draw, himself often a reformed gunman, the citizens saw to it they had order. The names of Wild Bill Hickok, Bat Masterson and Wyatt Earp became famous in the annals of lawmen, if about the only law these men knew was that of the "peacemaker" and "the equalizer", the pearl-handled six-shooting revolver.

Lawlessness reached such a point in Abilene that the town fathers became utterly disgusted. In February, 1872, they sent word to the Texans that they were no longer welcome and that in no circumstances were they to bring cattle to town. The cowboys cheered. Ellsworth

Left Homesteaders were a tough, resolute and uncompromising lot and were to prove more than a match for the cattlemen who tried to discourage them by tearing down their fences and driving their cattle over their land
Below *Hard Winter* by W.H.D. Koerner recalls the disastrous blizzard of 1886 when many cattle and cowboys died

had just opened up. It was new and it was sparkling. Smiling, the drovers simply turned their herds westward, at which the men of Abilene had second thoughts. Quite obviously, they had cut their very lifeline. Dumbstruck at their hasty stupidity, they rushed another emissary to the cowboys to invite them back. The cowboys just smiled again.

As Abilene sank into deserved oblivion, Ellsworth bloomed. But as the railroad expanded westward, Ellsworth died, too. Now Dodge City flourished, soon to become the cowboy capital.

While the former cow towns could attribute their demise to the westward thrust of the railroads, Dodge City collapsed for another reason. The winter of 1886 brought to the Plains the worst blizzard men could remember. Frigid winds blew snow high in great white drifts, covering the earth and filling the valleys. And with it all, thousands upon thousands of cows were buried and frozen stiff. When the spring thaws came, carcasses were found scattered everywhere. The cattle industry was in ruins. Everyone went broke and so did Dodge City. And so ended the fabulous era of the great Longhorn cattle drives and the legendary cow towns. For all its sheriffs, it just took one good snowstorm to clean up the sin and hypocrisy of the glittering cowboy capital.

Trail driving was not the cowboys' only occupation. Some men like John Chisum and Charles Goodnight established huge spreads in New Mexico. John Iliff controlled a hundred miles of water along the Platte where his cattle grazed on either side of the river as far as they could range. Free grass was the key to the size of these tremendous ranches. Men who could pin down water rights, sometimes with legal title, other times as squatters, could control vast stretches of grazing land. Some ranches encompassed hundreds of square miles and running a herd numbering ten thousand head was not uncommon.

Top left The "Varieties Saloon" Dodge City in the 1880s
Left Texas cowboys in a saloon during the 1890s
Above Dodge City, the flourishing cowboy capital. The terrible blizzard of 1886 heralded its ruin

Some ranges were so huge that the cowboys assigned to "ride the line" really couldn't keep track of the cattle. While the problem of strays was always bothersome, the matter of thievery was serious. Ranchers endeavored to protect their property by branding their cattle. Brands were individual marks burned on the hide with a red-hot iron. When ownership changed, the cow would receive another brand, that of the new owner. Some cows exchanged hands so many times that they took on the appearance of walking signboards. But branding did not prevent rustling. Cattle thieves were ingenious and one of their skills was the altering of brands. They used either a straight or "running iron" or preferably a short copper wire to do the job. Changing the wrench brand to the bit wasn't too difficult, nor was making 701 out of 10 or ROB from 701 beyond them. And the disguise worked, for it was pretty hard to prove a brand had been doctored. Ranchers took a dim view of cattle thieves. When caught in the act of changing a brand, the cattleman might take the culprit to town for trial, but he might not. Many a rustler was shot on the spot or invited to a "necktie party" to be hung by the neck from the nearest tree limb. The law of the West was often to shoot first and ask questions later.

If rustlers were a curse to the cowmen, the sheepmen were a plague. Sheepmen had as much right to the free grass as did the cattlemen, but not according to the ranchers. They argued not only that they had arrived first, but that the grazing habits of the sheep damaged the range. It is true that sheep crop the grass extremely close and when the roots are exposed to the searing rays of the western sun, the range burns out. A burned-out range meant thin cows, and thin cows spelled shrunken profits. This the ranchers would not accept. Cowboys were simply ordered to go shoot sheep, and shoot sheep they did, sometimes as many as a thousand or more in a single day. And when their grizzly job was done, when the ill-smelling "bleaters" could no longer harm the

grass, then the cowboys shot the sheepherders.

All this does not imply that the sheepmen didn't fight back. In Tonto Country, Arizona, the cattle-raising Graham family set up a "deadline" beyond which the Tweksbury clan's sheep might not pass. But the Tweksburys were not about to abide by the arbitrary boundaries established by the Grahams. They decided to graze their sheep where they damn well pleased. This, quite understandably, antagonized the Grahams. The result was the start of a nice little feud. Cowboys were bushwacked, sheepmen were dry-gulched. Lynchings were not uncommon. It all began in 1887, and in the five years the hostilities lasted, twenty-six men became corpses. It didn't end until the last surviving Graham was done in by the sole remaining Tweksbury. For this the sheepmen could raise a flag.

Top Cowboys on the rampage in Charles Russell's *In Without Knocking*
Above A cardsharp gets his just deserts in W.H.D. Koerner's *No Luck on the Draw*
Top right *Smoke of a .45* by Charles Russell—a frequent way of settling a feud

Still worse than even rustlers and the pioneering settlers were the men who grubbed for a living on their perky hundred-and-sixty-acre homesteads, who as "sodbusters" plowed up the range, who fenced their little "nests", depriving the cattlemen of their pre-empted free grass. Many of the nesters had legitimate government claims, others were mere squatters. No matter, to the cattlemen they were intruders and a threat. Again the cowmen retaliated. They cut the fences and drove their cows over the settlers' crops. Not a few "little gray homes in the west" were burned out. The homesteaders, however, were as determined as they were numerous and challenged the cattlemen for their right to the land. Johnson County, Wyoming, in the 1890s presents a pretty good picture of the conflict and the fun everyone was having.

Many of the great western spreads were owned by eastern interests, some as distant as Great Britain. Many of the cattle barons visited their empires perhaps only once or twice a year. Small ranchers, often nesters themselves, were jealous of the rich and powerful cattle kings and took action against them. By this time the large landholders had accepted barbed wire. Miles and miles of fencing was strung, serving as a means of preventing cattle from "drifting" and mixing with neighboring herds. The small ranchers gleefully cut the drift fences, thus allowing the cattle to escape. As if that weren't impertinence enough, the settlers took pleasure in branding any mavericks they found as well as altering brands to suit themselves. For the "little fellas" of Johnson County, rustling became a way of life. Even the cowboys working for the "big boys" were often a "little on the rustle," their loyalties being with the underdog. Men who remained faithful to their absentee owners were sneeringly referred to as "pliers men" because they spent so much of their time mending the fences the rustlers cut.

The ranches really were too big for men to patrol them effectively. And catching a rustler, even red-handed, was to little purpose. Brought to trial in Buffalo, the county seat, more often than not the culprits were promptly acquitted. This was understandable since the judge had been elected by his friends and neighbors, the very men on trial. The big ranchers really were hurting, their pockets no longer jingled with silver dollars. At last they decided to take matters in hand.

At Cheyenne, Wyoming, a meeting of cattle barons was held in April of 1892. Calling themselves the Regulators' Association, they hired some professional gunslingers and formed themselves into a little army of some forty men. Major Frank Wolcott was chosen captain. They planned to teach the Johnson County rustlers a thing or two and put a stop to their depredations. Taking a train to Casper, they unloaded their gear, weapons and horses at dawn and then boldly set out on their campaign to Buffalo, the core of all the festering.

The first place they came to was the Kay Cee, a ranch owned by Nathan Champion. He was a known rustler and, worse yet, an organizer of the "Settlers," the small ranchers' answer to the Regulators. Hiding among the barns and corrals, the Regulators waited. Shortly, a figure carrying a bucket appeared at the cabin door and walked toward the barns for water. He was immediately ambushed. The Regulators pumped him and learned that he and another trapper, Ben Jones, were staying the night whith Champion and his partner Nick Ray. Pretty soon Ben Jones stepped out of the door heading for the barn. He, too, facing a row of Winchester barrels, was captured without a fight. After a while Nick Ray came out to see why the trappers hadn't brought back the water. His curiosity was

Ladies' Satchels, large variety, at Emerton's.

MRS. LAUGHLIN.

P. O. Address, La Junta.

Earmarks, swallow-fork right, overbit and underbit left.

Horse brands, M on left shoulder and hip.

LANE & MURRAY.

P. O. Address, West Las Animas, Colo.

Range, Fort Lyon to Mud Creek.

Earmarks, underslope and underbit each ear.

Additional brands: Triangle on jaw, [brand] left loin, V right side, Pd left side, FS left side, 22 left side
Horse brand: HL on left shoulder.

MACEY & SYDNER.

P. O. Address, West Las Animas.

Earmarks, under half crop, both.

Other brands:

SIZR on right side,

JPM on left side.

Finest Brands of Cigars at Emerton's.

rewarded by a barrage of fire. Riddled in the head and chest, he tried to drag himself into the cabin as Champion came to his rescue. As he hauled his wounded partner to safety, Champion kept up a steady fire, wounding one of the Texas gunmen.

The siege which began in the early morning continued intermittently until mid-afternoon. In the meantime, Champion had wounded two more of his assailants, but sadly, about noon, his friend Nick Ray had died. It was about three o'clock that a settler named Black Jack Flagg rode up on horseback along with his young nephew who was driving a buckboard. Just in time they spotted the action. Hurriedly, Flagg and the boy unharnessed the horse, left the wagon and, under fire, made a hasty retreat toward Buffalo.

By now the day was wearing on and the Regulators had done little save get themselves wounded. Indecision would probably best describe their battle plan. At last, however, someone, stumbled on a masterly stratagem. Loading Mr. Flagg's wagon with sticks and brush, they set fire to it and pushed it up against Champion's cabin, where the flames began to do what the forty stalwart Regulators should have done much earlier. As the heat got more intense and the cabin filled with smoke, Champion was forced to make a move. Blazing away as he burst from the door, he was ripped up and down by gunfire.

Champion, however, left his mark. Almost un-

Below left An old Colorado brand book illustrates some of the many methods employed in cattle branding
Above In the eyes of the rancher sheepmen were as unpopular as cattle thieves
Below Cowboys branding cattle in the 1890s

believably, he kept a running account of the entire skirmish. The last line in his little black book read, "The house is all fired. Goodbye boys, if I never see you again."

The Regulators left their mark, too. They pinned a big note on the slain Champion's chest. CATTLE THIEVES BEWARE.

Flushed with victory, the conquerors rode heroically on toward Buffalo. They had seventy names on their list to take care of. From the length of time it had taken them to deal with Champion, the campaign was going to take about a month. They had ridden only as far as the TA Ranch, some fourteen miles south of Buffalo, when their forward scout, Phil Defrau, cantered up. Hastily he gave his report. The Regulators stopped dead in their tracks.

A band of settlers, seventy in all, was riding and riding hard in their direction. From the weapons they were brandishing, it was obvious they meant business. Black Jack Flagg had got word to Sheriff Red Angus in good time. News spread rapidly. Possemen appeared voluntarily at the sheriff's office. It was their necks or else. Red Angus was kept pretty busy deputizing the men and his supply of tin badges was sorely taxed.

For the Regulators, this was the moment of truth, their world had just been turned upside down. Outnumbered nearly two to one, this time they were motivated to a quick decision. Into the barn at the T A Ranch they scurried and tried to barricade themselves. The hunters were now the hunted. Strangely, the thought of attacking seems not to have entered Major Wolcott's head. Courage seemed to drain from the men like water through a sieve.

In no time the posse had reached the T A Ranch and

wasted not a moment in giving the Regulators a taste of their own medicine. In the shadows of the Big Horn Mountains to the west, the settlers fired on the barn. Shots were exchanged. As more and more recruits assembled, the posse, unlike the Regulators, were quick to push flaming wagons filled with hay against the barn. The men from Cheyenne were about to learn the lesson they so loved to teach—how it feels to fry.

Just as the end of the Regulators was about to become a reality, the brassy sound of a bugle was heard in the distance. Suddenly over the horizon a troop of U. S. Cavalry appeared, then another and another. In less time than it took to burn the barn, the troops had everything under control, stopped the fighting and spoiled all the fun. The Johnson County war was over almost before it started.

Trouble flared in New Mexico, too, especially along the Pecos River. Two willful men, each with a reputation that smelled like a dead cow, were the cause of the publicized Lincoln County War. John Chisum, having got out of Texas in debt to the tune of ninety thousand dollars, carved out for himself a ranch in Lincoln county the size of Pennsylvania. He had so many cows, some hundred thousand of them, that his cowboys could barely keep track of them. Chisum's cattle were branded with the famous "long rail," a bar running from flank to shoulder. Their ears were marked with cuts, giving them the appearance of having four ears and the nickname "jingle bob." One of the reasons Chisum's men couldn't get their count right was because

Below *Stampede* by Frederic Remington. Sometimes a herd of cattle could stampede as many as six times in one night

Major Frank Wolcott   Red Angus   Billy the Kid

his cattle were being rustled and Chisum was being robbed blind. When thieves were caught, they miraculously escaped jail.

Major L. G. Murphy of Lincoln owned the general store, the saloon, the bank and the town's sheriff. He also owned a small ranch. People wondered how he managed to sell so many steers, but no one dared challenge him. No one, that is, but Chisum, who flatly accused Murphy to his face. Murphy merely laughed. He did, however, employ Alexander McSween, a young lawyer, to represent him.

John Tunstall was a very wealthy Englishman lured to the West by its ruggedness and stark beauty. He bought himself a spread near Lincoln and hired a bunch of cowhands, including an affable young boy named William Bonney.

It all began one day when some of Murphy's cowboys were caught hands down stealing Chisum's cattle. Murphy ordered McSween to defend his thieves, but McSween refused. The culprits were too obviously guilty and the young attorney was one of those rare members of the bar with a sense of principle. Murphy was as livid as he was helpless.

Not long afterward, John Chisum retained McSween to protect his interests. He still had his Texas creditors to worry about. As if that weren't move enough to anger Murphy, the genial Tunstall decided to open a general store in Lincoln, neatly jeopardizing Murphy's monopoly. Worse yet, he hired McSween to run the business. The next slap in the face for Murphy was when Chisum, using Tunstall's money, opened a bank at the rear of the Tunstall store. But even that wasn't all. Murphy was contesting an inheritance case, claiming that the money belonged to him. Alexander McSween, defying his former employer, ruled in favor of the rightful heir, courting Murphy's further wrath, by transferring the property to Tunstall's trust.

Reaction was electric. Murphy sent a posse to the Tunstall ranch with orders to confiscate the Englishman's cattle in sufficient numbers to compensate for what Murphy had lost in the inheritance. Moreover, they were to bring in Tunstall as well.

At first the Englishman refused to accompany Murphy's posse, but finally he agreed. Tunstall was no sugarplum. With him he took his cowhands, who rode ahead. Some of the possemen were half-drunk. Along the way a shot rang out. William Bonney, Tunstall's cowboy, looked back, horrified to see his boss and benefactor fall dead from his saddle. Then and there the unlikely-looking cowboy mentally ticked off the names of every posse member and vowed to wreak vengeance. What's more, he could make it stick, for in reality Bonney was none other than Billy the Kid, one of the West's most deadly shots and wanton killers.

Now the conflict took on all the aspects of guerrilla warfare. Chisum and McSween were fortunate to have Billy the Kid on their side, but Murphy was quick to hire gunslingers of his own. As the months passed, small bands of armed men patrolled the countryside. Cowboys were dry-gulched, sheriffs bushwacked.

Matters took a more decisive turn in Lincoln when the Murphy forces discovered they had McSween and his

men cornered in McSween's house, and with it the chance to settle the score once and for all. So the Murphy men set fire to the house with the object of smoking out the enemy. And smoke them out they did. Mrs. McSween and some women friends were the first to be forced to leave. Not one shot was fired as the ladies walked down the street. When McSween and some other men stepped over the threshold, it was a different game. They were instantly gunned down in a hail of lead. Finally, Billy the Kid and his followers could stand the heat no longer. Bursting through the doorway, they zigzagged up and down the street and by a stroke of luck escaped. The Kid was the last to leave. Blazing away with his firearms, he wounded two and killed one of his assailants and made his getaway unscathed.

With McSween's death, the Lincoln County War became the Kid's personal vendetta. Every man in Murphy's posse was already a corpse or his days were numbered. But the Kid's days were numbered, too. Pat Garrett, the new sheriff of Lincoln County, had the principal assignment of bringing in the Kid. And Garrett was relentless. On the night of July 14, 1881, Pat courageously ambushed Billy in a darkened bedroom on the Maxwell ranch. Billy the Kid, who had killed twenty-one men by the age of twenty-one, was now himself a customer for the undertaker.

Pat Garrett's brave act brought the Lincoln County War to a bloody end. Murphy, bankrupt from paying so many Texas killers, died before he knew the outcome. Chisum left the county and they dug his grave three years later in Arkansas.

Left to right Major Frank Wolcott fought a running battle against rustlers in the Johnson County War. Red Angus was prepared to deputize anyone. Billy the Kid was twenty-one when he was shot dead. Dapper-looking Pat Garrett hunted down Billy the Kid and ended the Johnson County War. John H. Tunstall, the wealthy Englishman, was a victim of the Lincoln County War. Rancher John Chisum's feud with Major J.L. Murphy sparked off the Lincoln County War

Not all cowboys were clean-living, hardworking young men who lived a lonely life on the trail and had a good time when they came to town. Some cowboys were rotten. John Hardin was one of them.

Born in Fanin County, Texas, in 1853, John Wesley Hardin was the son of a circuit-riding Methodist preacher. At the end of the Civil War, Texas, as was true of all the South, was victimized by Yankee carpetbaggers and haughty free negroes. In many instances these meddlers took over the reins of local government, much to the chagrin of the natives. It was in 1868 that "Wess" Hardin first ran afoul of the situation. According to Wess, he was being clubbed to death by a burly negro named Maze, and to save himself he shot and killed the black man. Realizing his chance of acquittal in the Yankee-dominated courts was nil, Wess ran away. Pursued by two white officers and a negro, Wess got the drop on all three and buried them under the sand. Having wiped out four men at the age of fifteen, the boy was well on the road to a great career in killing.

In 1869 he pumped lead into another white officer and shortly after downed his sixth victim, Jim Bradly, in a gambling dispute. Number seven was a circus man who threatened to mash in his face while number eight demanded a hundred dollars from what he took to be an ingenuous boy. Wess's slug hit the man squarely between the eyes.

Wess was finally captured and jailed for killing a Mr. Hoffman, a murder, in fact, he did not commit. While being transported to trial, Wess escaped, killing deputy Sheriff Jim Smalley in the process with a little pistol concealed under his armpit. Apprehended again, he was held under guard by three Texas state officers, Smith, Davis and Jones. All three died as Wess's gun spat fire and he could now count twelve notches on his stock.

Later, while driving twelve hundred Longhorns on the Chisholm Trail toward Abilene, Wess shot two

Above Belle Starr did a brisk trade in stolen horses and kept open house for rustlers and outlaws
Right Calamity Jane looks as though she could handle herself in a tough spot but a far cry from the later celluloid images that were to follow many of the famous and infamous names the West produced

Indians, one for demanding toll. A little farther along the trail he got into a row with some Mexican cowhands. He settled that squabble by spilling the blood of five of them all over the prairie.

In Abilene he was confronted by Sheriff Wild Bill Hickok who got the draw on him. Pointing his pistol at Hardin's head, Hickok ordered the boy to hand over his two weapons. Wess offered the pistols, handle first, with the barrels pointing toward himself. As Hickok lowered his aim to reach for the guns, Wess suddenly spun them around and instantly aimed both at the sheriff's head. By sheer dint of personal dominance, Hickok talked Wess into surrendering his arms. Then on the boy's promise that he would behave himself, Hickok offered him his friendship and a drink. Wess obeyed. Hickok showed the youngster a Texas warrant for his arrest but agreed not to serve it so long as they were friends. And friends indeed they remained. Hickok even deputized Hardin to apprehend a missing Mexican murderer. Wess punctured him in a café on the Kansas border. When the body was brought in, the cattlemen raised a thousand-dollar purse as Hardin's reward.

But Hardin couldn't seem to stay out of trouble and didn't seem to want to. Drinking in a saloon with a friend and hearing some ruffians making derogatory comments about Texans. Wess advised them he was a Texan. Shooting broke out. Wess settled the argument by plugging the leader, but left town at a gallop.

This was the story of Wess Hardin's life. Either he was defending himself, avenging a friend's death, running and hiding from the law or catching odd jobs as a wrangler. As time went on, the list of victims steadily increased. The gory roster included, in addition to the first twenty-one men he had mowed down, two sheriffs, four Texas state policemen, J. B. Morgan, four negro policemen, one Mexican holdup man, one sneak thief, one negro gunslinger and two unknown roughnecks whom he shot in the dark. This was a grand total of thirty-seven men, though some authorities said the

Indians didn't count. Hardin managed to accomplish all this bloodshed by the time he was twenty-two.

How he could so long have escaped his captors seems unbelievable. But in Texas of the 1870s he had many friends and relatives who were happy to hide him out against the northern-controlled courts. In July of 1877, however, his luck ran out. Enjoying a big black cigar in a smoking car, he was captured from behind by Texas Ranger John Armstrong. At his trial he pleaded that he had never killed a man except in self-defense. The jury somehow saw it otherwise and sent him up the river for twenty-five years.

Hardin spent sixteen years in jail and busied himself studying law. Upon his release, he hung out his shingle in El Paso as a practicing attorney. And then on the night of August 19, 1895, he and a friend were gambling. Sheriff John Selman, with whom Hardin had quarreled earlier that day, walked in. Selman wasted no time. He ended Hardin's legal practice instantly by filling the back of his head with lead.

Not all the bad men were men. Some, like Cattle Kate who got herself hung for rustling, and Calamity Jane, an uncouth, tobacco-chewing slut enamored of Wild Bill Hickok, were of the gentler sex. Belle Starr was as alluring as a hyena in heat with a face just like one to prove it. Born in Missouri, she waited until she was twenty-four before eloping with Jim Reed. It didn't bother Jim that Belle already had one son on the side. He himself had a fine reputation as a horse thief and stage robber, besides having at least one solid murder to his name. The love nest lasted two years and might have gone on longer had Jim not got himself shot dead while resisting an arresting officer.

Belle then opened a livery stable in Dallas where some of the horses she sold had a clean bill of sale, but the majority did not. Later she married a Cherokee Indian named Sam Starr and the two of them settled along the Canadian River. They ran a kind of hostelry in their cabin. It was a nice secluded place for cattle thieves and men running from the law to visit. Belle was not above stealing a horse now and again, but she and Sam were then caught themselves. For their clumsiness, they spent a quiet year from 1883–84 in the hoosegow. Two years later, Sam got into an argument with a peace officer. Belle's marriage ended then and there as Sam and the lawman did each other in. In 1889 Belle was riding her horse down a country road, minding her own business. A neighbor who had earlier accused Belle of rustling his stock, spied her and took a potshot. He was acquitted. Belle's daughter, Pearl, attended her funeral.

The role of the cattle industry in the development of the West was not just colorful, it was fundamental. Providing meat for the population was as valuable a contribution to the economy as were the crops the farmers harvested. It was a business fraught with arduous and often hazardous work, plagued by the vagaries of the weather and drained by thievery. It took men of stamina and courage willing to gamble against many odds to carry on a successful operation. As one character put it, "A cowboy is a man with guts and a horse."

THE EMPIRE BUILDERS

The discovery of gold led to an even greater rush West. The rich mining towns clamored for contact with the business centers in the East. Soon names like Wells Fargo, the Butterfield Stage and the Pony Express were to be heard, together with those of the new railroad companies.

Left The linking of the Union and Central Pacific Railroads at Promontory, Utah, May 10, 1869
Above Panning for gold by hand

JOHANN AUGUST SUTTER, born in Germany of Swiss parents in 1803, came to America at the age of 31. Reaching St. Louis, he had an urge to go farther, taking the Santa Fe Trail, he proceeded to California. Here he was soon successful in developing extensive trading interests along the coast and out into the Pacific as far as Hawaii. Later he established a community which he named New Helvetia. His own place, known as Sutter's Fort, became a haven for travelers, while his mills, livestock and agricultural holdings made him a wealthy and powerful man. And then, on January 19, 1849, Sutter's whole world changed.

J. W. Marshall, a partner in a sawmill project, found traces of gold in the millrace. Promptly reporting his find to Sutter, they together verified its genuineness. Sutter decided it was best to keep the whole matter a secret, but word got out and rumors spread. Almost overnight, shopkeepers left their stores, farmers dropped their plows and Sutter's Mill was overrun. News soon reached the East. Early in 1849, booklets were printed describing how to mine and how to get to California. Picks and shovels and pans sold like peanuts at a circus. The gold fever had struck the nation. The "forty-niners" began their rush.

There were several routes to California. The safest and most convenient was to take a sailing ship around Cape Horn. Aside from the monotony and the poor food, the chief disadvantage of going by water was that it took so long—six boring months. A shorter route was to go by sea to Panama, cross the isthmus and take another ship to California. The port cities of Colon and Panama, however, were filthy and the jungle was ridden with cholera and fever. So while it was quicker than sailing around the Horn, it was both more inconvenient and dangerous. The two principal overland routes were the Santa Fe and Oregon trails. Here the travelers faced all the hardships of their predecessors and more. In their frantic haste to start mining gold and get rich quick, they were often ill-equipped and physically soft. Unlike the pioneers before them who were already hardened to frontier life, many of the forty-niners were city people unaccustomed to the rigors of outdoor living. Sadly, their inexperience cost many lives.

San Francisco suddenly became a booming port. Not only did prospectors arriving by ship jam the city, but those gold seekers from overland congregated to refurbish their supplies. Sailors, abandoning their ships in favor of seeking gold, swelled the ranks. Lodgings were in short supply. A bunk in a tent might cost as much as twenty dollars a week, a room in a lodging house two hundred and fifty a month. Food, too, was high, sugar, for example, bringing three dollars a pound. Most purchases were made in gold dust and all shopkeepers had scales for weighing it.

The chance of easy riches attracted not only the prospectors, but others who hoped to find wealth from the miners themselves. Glittering saloons and dance halls flourished, and what gold these failed to drain from the miners' purses, the gambling halls did. The city became a haven for the professional gambler, the best-dressed man in town. Harlots, too, unabashedly plied their trade and houses of ill repute were common. Except for the dance hall girls, who were not usually prostitutes, the ladies of pleasure were about the only women in town. Crime ran high in San Francisco and murders were commonplace. Matters became so critical that a vigilante committee was formed. The committee, however, decided that crime paid and itself became an organizer of the criminal element. Not until 1851 was a new committee formed. It still took five years and another thousand murders before the city was cleaned up.

While San Francisco had its problems with crime, the countryside also had its share. The name Joaquin Murieta brought terror to ranchers, store owners, saloonkeepers and stagecoach passengers alike, for Joaquin was the leader of a gang of ruthless Mexican bandits. One of the members had the descriptive name of Three Fingered Jack. So much of a scourge was Joaquin that in 1853 the governor placed a reward of fifteen hundred dollars for him dead or alive. The gang was hard to find, added to which there happened to be not one, but five

Below left Rotting ships at San Francisco. Many seamen joined the gold rush leaving hundreds of vessels unmanned

Below Sutter's Fort—center of the wealthy New Helvetia community, destroyed by the discovery of gold

Bottom In nearly every mining town prostitutes operated from "cribs" such as these in Gold Field, Nevada and they did a roaring trade

Joaquins, a problem easily resolved in the event by the pursuing rangers. They simply captured the first gang they came upon. One of the members was Three Fingered Jack. They chopped off his hand and, assuming him to be their man, the leader's head. Both were pickled in jars of alcohol and exhibited in Sacramento as Joaquin's head and Three Finger's hand. Years later Joseph E. Badger, Jr. wrote a dime novel entitled *Joaquin the Terrible* which made the bandit out to be a sort of Robin Hood. While the book sold well, it could hardly be accused of sticking to the facts.

Early gold mining was something of a simpleton's task requiring a considerable amount of extremely hard work. Essential tools were a large pan, a pick and a shovel. Gold was found as pure nuggets by merely digging in the earth and along the stream banks or as dust in the stream beds themselves. In either case the sand and earth that was dug out was placed in the pan over which water was sloshed. In this manner the mud was cleared from the pan while the sand and gold, being heavier, remained in the bottom. When this combination was dried, the sand was simply blown away leaving pure gold. This was a one-man job and a miner could spend as many hours at it a day as his back could stand.

Other devices were developed using this same principle. A rocker, a kind of box with a screen, took the work of three men to operate, one to dump in the dirt, one to pour the water and one to operate the rocker. Later, hydraulic systems were designed utilizing sluices to carry the water. But no matter what method was employed, they all meant hard work and sore muscles.

At first most of the mining was done in and about the American and Sacramento rivers for it was in this area that men made the richest finds. It was on the American River that Sutter's Mill was located. His land was tramped over, dug up, and his cattle killed to a point where he faced financial ruin. Sutter was powerless to hold back the flood of miners. He finally went so far as to request Congress for indemnification, but that fell on the unsympathetic ears of the Supreme Court. Sutter left California in 1873 and moved to Pennsylvania utterly destroyed.

In 1849 it was estimated that a quarter of a million dollars' worth of gold was mined, four years later over eighty-one millions' worth was extracted. Yet it is interesting to note that few individuals attained great wealth. It has been reported that two men found seventeen thousand dollars' worth in a week, but that

was unusual. The average California gold miner dug up only four dollars' worth of gold a day, scarcely a way to get rich quick.

When gold became hard to find, the miners moved on to richer fields. News of a good discovery spread quickly and men swarmed to it hoping for better luck. They would form camps, composed mostly of tents and rude shacks. Then they set up rules, especially with respect to the size of individual claims, claim jumping and theft. Claims varied in size depending on the character of the land, but the largest was usually no more than a hundred by a hundred feet while ten by ten feet was not uncommon.

By 1857 the easy pickings had begun to peter out. Surface mining in California became less and less profitable for the independent miner. Only well-financed groups with large investments in expensive equipment could afford to continue. Now, however, men were searching all over the Rocky Mountain regions of the West for new finds. Nor were their efforts unrewarded. They did discover gold. Strikes had already been made in Nevada in 1855 and the miners flocked there. Farther east other discoveries were made in Idaho and later in Montana. By 1863, Virginia City was prominent and a year later Last Chance Gulch was an established mecca.

Left A dipper gold dredge in Central California during the 1890s
Above Placer mining on the San Juan River, Utah. The dredge and sluice box were better than pans but still no guarantee of riches. Gold brought riches to only a small number of stalwarts

Two of the greatest discoveries, however, occurred in Nevada and Colorado. It was in 1858 that William Green Russell made a strike on Little Dry Creek, a tributary of Cherry Creek some forty miles south of what is now Denver, thirty-five miles north of towering Pikes Peak. And with Russell's find, the gold rush began all over again. As a result of the panic of '57, many easterners were only too eager to grab at the chance of easy riches. This time the cry was "Pikes Peak or bust." Here, as in California, the miners at first merely grubbed the surface, hunting only for pure gold in the form of nuggets and dust. By now, however, most men were aware that the gold they found were mere particles washed down from a hidden "mother load" in the mountains. As more and more strikes were made in such places as Central City and Black Hawk, new and improved techniques were utilized. Fewer and fewer men were content simply to pick around on the surface. Instead, shafts were dug to reach the rich veins. Stamping mills and smelters were constructed to extract the gold from the rocky quartz it had originally intruded. Men were employed in the mines and a true industry boomed. Here was a bonanza, first in gold, then in silver, and it was here that some men grew fabulously wealthy.

Men like James G. Fair, John L. Routt, Bert Carlton and Nathaniel P. Hill became rich men almost over the weekend. Among them H. A. W. Tabor stands out as one of the more colorful.

Tabor was a Vermont stonecutter who came West in the 1860s. That was hard work, but he was successful in landing an easy job as postmaster in Leadville, Colorado. He also worked in and about the mines there for many years. And then one day in 1875 a couple of miners asked Tabor for a grubstake—seventeen dollars' worth of hope. In a few years the strike was worth enough for Tabor to sell it for a million dollars. With his money he bought the Matchless Mine and other property. The Matchless brought him in some eleven million dollars. Everything Tabor touched turned to silver. His wife, appropriately named Augusta, was prim, proper and penny-wise and bored Tabor stiff. He divorced her in favor of a "Kewpie doll" who looked exactly as if she were made of genuine celluloid. Everyone knew her as "Baby Doe." Anything Baby Doe wanted, Tabor bought for her. Even when she didn't need it, Tabor bought it for her—matched teams of horses, for instance, to go with her attire of the day.

Tabor's influence compounded with his wealth and in 1883 he was appointed to fill the unexpired term of Senator H. M. Teller. With his wealth and power, he was also flamboyantly generous. He gave both Leadville and Denver fabulous opera houses, the Denver Grand considered by some the most elegant of its day. And then all the splendor, the ostentatious lavishness to which he and Baby Doe had become accustomed, disintegrated in less time than it takes gold dust tc settle in a pan. The Depression of 1893 rendered Tabor practically penniless. He lost nearly everything he owned. His political friends took pity on him and bailed him out to some extent. As a political hack, he was appointed to the dunderhead's job he knew, this time as postmaster of Denver, a position he held for six years. Luckily, death relieved him from the boredom of the most comfortable government job ever conceived. On his deathbed he implored Baby Doe to "hold onto the Matchless." This she did. While the mine never produced enough silver to buy a postage stamp, Baby Doe faithfully guarded an empty dream in a rickety shack for thirty-six years. Here, in 1935, she was found in rags, frozen to death.

Besides the paltry return for time and energy spent and the possibility of going completely broke, mining held other hazardous surprises. Lone prospectors were not infrequently attacked and killed by Indians, others fell down shafts or were crushed to death by cave-ins. One fate, however, that few miners figured on was

Commercial advertisements with noble exhortations such as these tempted many to seek their fortunes in the West and made a fortune for Levi Strauss who had the right clothes for just about everyone

devised by an Alfred E. Packer. Prospecting in the mountains of Colorado with his friends Israel Swan, George Noon, Frank Miller, James Humphreys and Wilson Bell, he and the party were stranded in a blizzard. Food ran out and the chance of rescue was nil. Alfred and his companions got hungry, but Alfred was the hungriest. So he butchered his pals with his little axe and ate them up one by one.

Later, when the remains of his repast were discovered, Packer was apprehended and brought to trail. It has been said that in pronouncing sentence the judge, himself a Democrat, not only chastised Packer for his heinous mass murder, but savagely tongue-lashed him for his even more evil offense—that in a county with only seven Democrats he had had the audacity to consume five of them! There is a bronze plaque to Packer's victims but our hero Alfred's name does not appear.

Gold was not the only resource which the westerners sought. Timber was another rich target. Loggers were already cutting in Wisconsin by the 1830s. Minnesota and later Washington, Oregon and California were seemingly inexhaustible sources. While domestic demands were large, foreign markets for ships' timbers were equally great. The lumberjacks' work was hard and dangerous, but the rewards were worth the risks. And like the fur traders, no one dreamed that by the end of the century the forests would be cut to the point of devastation.

Communication between the East and West before the advent of the mining towns was sporadic, haphazard and extremely difficult. In fact, it was all but nonexistent. Letters and newspapers were carried West by immigrants and freighters. Letters were often mailed in cabins and even in the crotches of trees, much to the diversion of passers-by, for while a thoughtful traveler might generously carry it toward its destination, everyone had fun reading the letter first. Even so, it was better to have a letter publicized than have it not reach its destination at all. At best, however, probably only half those mailed ever got through.

The first regular mail to reach San Francisco came by the Pacific Mail Steamship Company's boat on

Top left A Concord Wagon in the 1880s. The stage-coaches made at Concord, New Hampshire were famed for rough cross-country travel

Bottom left *Indians Attacking a Stage* by H.W. Hansen

Below Statue commemorating the Pony Express, which ran a service between St Joseph and Placerville, California—almost 2,000 miles—every day

Bottom Overland House, Idaho—a welcome resting place for weary travelers on the Overland Trail

February 22, 1849. This coincided neatly with the gold rush, so much so that every last sailor jumped ship. The company finally got sailing again with bimonthly deliveries at fifty cents a letter.

As the needs of the California mining communities grew and the necessity of getting the gold and letters of credits to the banks increased, so did the demand for improved transportation. By 1852, Alvin Adams had formed the Adams and Company Express to meet just that need in California. Henry Wells and William Fargo knew a good thing when they saw it and founded a competing company, the Wells Fargo. The Santa Fe trade had already proved feasible. Now pack trains and freighters went on from Santa Fe to El Paso and then north to California. The Oregon Trail was also used, now dropping south to Salt Lake City and over the Sierras. The trip was an interminably long one, in some instances dangerous and always wearisomely slow. It took the mule teams thirty days to get from Council Bluffs to Salt Lake City and another thirty days from Salt Lake to California. Slow as it was, it was big business. The Butterfield freighting operation involved over six thousand wagons and seventy-five thousand oxen.

Despite the westerners' demands for mail service, it took the postmaster general until 1857 to call finally for bids. John Butterfield of the American Express Company and William Fargo of Wells Fargo Express, together with four other men, founded the Butterfield Overland Stage and received the contract. But only in 1858 did the stages begin running. From St. Louis to Little Rock, south to Preston and El Paso, the route continued to Yuma and on to San Francisco. It was a distance of twenty-seven hundred and fifty miles and the stages made it in twenty days, an average of over a hundred and thirty-five miles a day.

The stagecoaches, Concord Wagons made in Concord, New Hampshire, were pulled by a team of six horses for ten-mile hauls to "swing stations", where worn-out horses were exchanged for fresh ones, and jostled passengers could stretch a leg. The stages traveled day and night with periodic stopovers at "home stations." Here the herds of horses were corralled, and food, mostly rancid bacon, stale bread and bitter coffee, was served the travelers. Having paid a two-hundred-dollar fare, such tasty meals were naturally to be expected. The roads were sometimes so rough as to be almost impassable. Sleep was a matter of catnaps, though if there was no excess baggage, ladies might sleep on the stagecoach floor. No food or water was served between home stations though passengers were permitted to bring their own snacks and whiskey, which most did. After twenty days of being jostled in a swinging, swerving coach, of being either drenched by rain or smothered in dust, eating poor food and drinking bad whiskey, the survivors of such a trip were usually a

Left The Stages of the Wells Fargo Company were popular targets for holdup men
Below C.E. Bolton was the real name of the poet-bandit better known as "Black Bart"
Right This "Wanted" poster had no effect. A detective was needed to arrest this particular "road agent"

☛ Agents of W., F. & Co. will not post this circular, but place them in the hands of your local and county officers, and reliable citizens in your region. Officers and citizens receiving them are respectfully requested to preserve them for future reference.

Agents WILL PRESERVE a copy on file in their office.

$800.00 Reward!

ARREST STAGE ROBBER!

1.

On the 3d of August, 1877, the stage from Fort Ross to Russian River was stopped by one man, who took from the Express box about $300, coin, and a check for $305.52, on Grangers' Bank of San Francisco, in favor of Fisk Bros. The Mail was also robbed. On one of the Way Bills left with the box the Robber wrote as follows:—

"I've labored long and hard for bread—
For honor and for riches—
But on my corns too long you've trod,
You fine haired sons of bitches.
BLACK BART, the P o 8.

Driver, give my respects to our friend, the other driver; but I really had a notion to hang my old disguise hat on his weather eye." (*fac simile.*)

Respectfully
B. B

It is believed that he went to the Town of Guerneville about daylight next morning.

2.

About one year after above robbery, July 25th, 1878, the Stage from Quincy to Oroville was stopped by one man, and W., F. & Co's box robbed of $379. coin, one Diamond Ring, (said to be worth $200) one Silver Watch, valued at $25. The Mail was also robbed. In the box, when found next day, was the following, (*fac simile*):—

here I lay me down to sleep
to wait the coming morrow
perhaps success perhaps defeat
And everlasting sorrow
I've labored long and hard for bread
for honor and for riches
But on my corns too long you've tred
You fine haired sons of bitches
let come what will I'll try it on
My condition can't be worse
and if there's money in that Box
Tis munny in my purse
Black Bart
the Po8

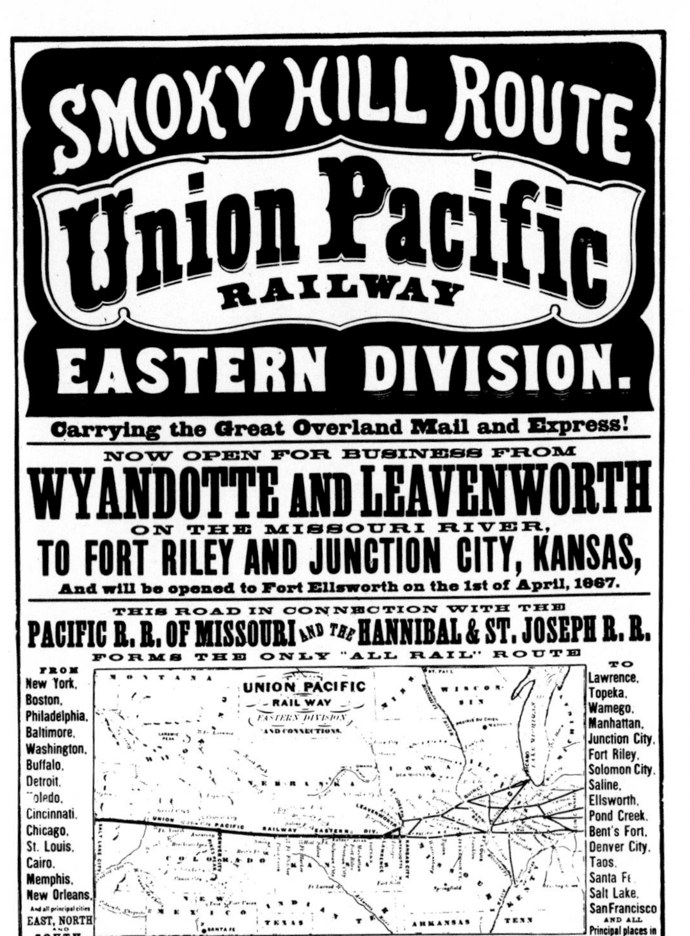

Left New vistas opened up and immense profits flowed in with the opening in 1867 of the Union Pacific Railroad's Eastern service

Below A crew laying a section of track on the Union Pacific Railroad. Crews were made up of men from literally every corner of the world: Irishmen, Europeans and even Chinese laborers

Top A logging train. There seemed to be a limitless supply of timber in the West and no attempt was made at reforestation—with dire consequences

Right Breaking a log jam. A lumberjack's work was dangerous but well paid. The railroad was of course one of the most demanding customers as with every mile of new track timber was required for ties and the construction of bridges

pretty haggard, bedraggled and often soused group of travelers. There were two compensations. The stage often got through and the scenery was lovely.

While the Butterfield Stage ran a southern route, Russell, Majors and Waddell traveled a central road. This ran along the Platte to Julesburg and on West. Like the Butterfield Overland Company, the coaches were drawn by four to six horses. Drivers sat atop the stage. These "ribbon handlers" were men of skill, strength and courage. Often they were accompanied by a guard "riding shotgun." Stagecoaches were subject to both Indian attack and "road agents." These bandits took great pleasure in commandeering the "box," the chest containing money and valuables, as well as relieving the passengers of their best belongings.

One of the more imaginative holdup men was Black Bart. Armed with a shotgun and wearing a white duster and a hood fashioned from a flour sack, he stuck up some twenty-eight stages. Black Bart had a flair for writing pretty poetry which he left at the scene as a kind of trademark. One of his better efforts went as follows:

I've labored long and hard for bread,
For honor and for riches.
But on my corns too long you've tred,
You fine-haired sons-of-bitches.

Black Bart The P O 8

The Wells Fargo Company, victims of too many of his robberies as well as fed up with his doggerel, finally set up an eight-hundred-dollar reward. And then Black Bart, in addition to committing crimes, committed a small oversight. Near the scene of one of his holdups he left a couple of bags of stale crackers, three dirty linen cuffs and a crumpled handkerchief. The handkerchief contained a telltale laundry mark: FX07. Supplied with this clue, detective J. B. Hume, a gumshoe for Wells Fargo, went to work. After doggedly spot-checking over ninety laundries in San Francisco, he finally found the mark belonged to a prosperous and well-dressed miner named C. E. Bolton. The game was up. Mr. Bolton was charged, convicted, and for several years enjoyed fresh crackers at the taxpayers' expense in San Quentin penitentiary.

Even with the stagecoaches rushing back and forth from the Coast, the Californians still clamored for faster mail service. Senator Gwin of California is credited with the suggestion that a relay of horsemen could carry the mail through in a good deal less time than the horse-drawn Concords. Russell, Majors and Waddell were quick to buy the idea and promptly received a contract to execute it. It was dubbed the "Pony Express" and proved to be not only efficient, but one of the more ingenious contributions to the making of the West. A hundred and ninety way stations were set up about ten miles apart on the nearly two-thousand-mile run from St. Joseph to Placerville, California. To reduce the weight, only small men and boys were selected as riders. To lighten the burden further, they were permitted to carry only two colt revolvers, even though parts of the route traversed hostile Indian country. Forty to ninety letters were carried wrapped in oiled silk and stuffed into leather saddlebags. The cost for mailing was five dollars per ounce.

Riders changed mounts every ten miles and each rider covered between seventy and a hundred miles before he was relieved. In the case of a rider's sickness or injury, another man might have to take a double turn. William Cody once rode continuously for twenty hours to cover three hundred and twenty miles. His record was surpassed by "Pony Bob" who covered three hundred and eighty miles nonstop. Riders were indeed as courageous as they were hardy and for the pounding they took were well paid. Novices got as much as $1.6 a day, experienced veterans received $5.

The first run was made on April 3, 1860. The riders made it in ten and a half days, just half the time that it took the stagecoaches. The venture was a complete success and hailed as another milestone in the conquest of the West. And then in October, 1861, telegraph lines sent their first tickings across the nation. Within a year

Below The Missouri steamboat "De Smet" tied up at Fort Benton, Montana c. 1870

and a half of its beginning, the glamorous Pony Express became as useless as a dead horse. The founders, Russell, Majors and Waddell, promptly went bankrupt.

Much competition existed between the big stage and freighting companies and their promoters. The panic of 1855 ruined Alvan Adams, and Wells Fargo took over. An uneducated sloven named Ben Holliday finally bought out Russell, Majors and Waddell when they went broke in 1862, their contract not having been renewed. By 1866, Holliday controlled five thousand miles of stage lines from Utah to Montana and all the country between. He apparently never tried to acquire his chief competitor, Wells Fargo, possibly because so many of their boxes got stolen. Instead, sensing the imminence of the Pacific Railroad's destruction of his own business, he sold his holdings to Wells Fargo. For all Holliday's insight and remarkable organizational ability, his great wealth and power, he was still by any standards an unmitigated boor.

One of the earliest, most common, most dependable and least expensive modes of transportation was the river traffic. The French *coureurs de bois* were quick to adopt the Indians' canoe. This was a conveyance for transporting furs from the Northwest to Montreal. Using both birchbark and dugout, voyageurs could traverse the close to five thousand miles of waterways carrying from three to eight tons of goods within a hundred days. Lewis and Clark made their journey as far as the mouth of the Marias in a bateau equipped with twenty-two oars, a sail and two piragnes. They could make about fifteen miles a day upstream, more often than not tugging it with ropes along the shore.

Flatboats were in common use. They were, in reality, mere forty-foot-long boxes with a twelve-foot beam, an eight-foot depth and drew practically no water at all. Usually equipped with four thirty-foot oars, a fifty-foot tiller and often a sail, they were great for downstream navigation. The keelboat, slightly less cumbersome than the bargelike flatboat, was fifty feet long and twelve feet wide with a tapering prow and keel. These boats not only carried oars and a sail, but were fitted with a platform at the gunwale. Men standing on this plunged one end of long poles into the river bottom, walked forward pushing the pole and thus propelled the boat. When the last man on the platform reached the forward position, he removed his pole and returned to the aft position and again began his walk. Keelboats could carry up to forty tons of freight and every man who pushed a pole could guarantee it.

West of the Mississippi two other types of boats were popular. The "Mackinaw" was a fifty-foot rowboat with a five-foot bow and stern and a three-foot midsection where the cargo was stored. At the forward section were four oarsmen, while a helmsman guided the craft with an oar from the aft deck. Most unwieldy was the "bullboat," originally used by the Missouri River Indians. This was composed of a series of bent willow rods lashed together to form a dome, over which were stretched buffalo hides. Sewn together, the seams

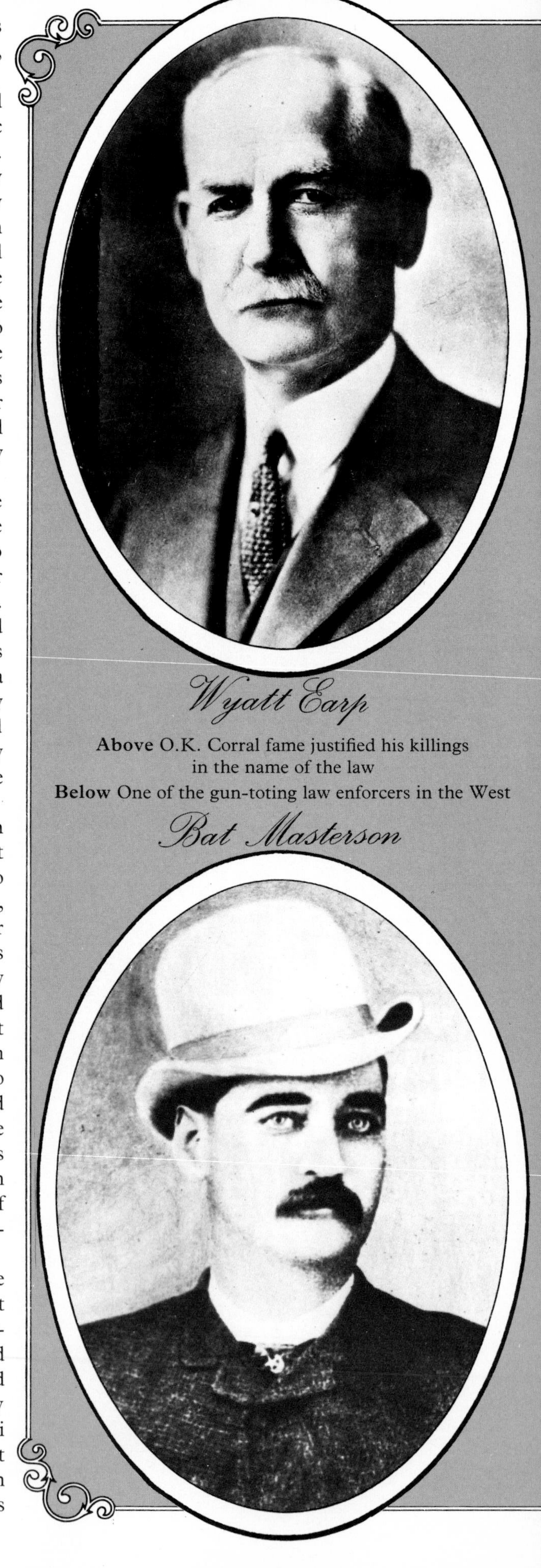

Above O.K. Corral fame justified his killings in the name of the law
Below One of the gun-toting law enforcers in the West

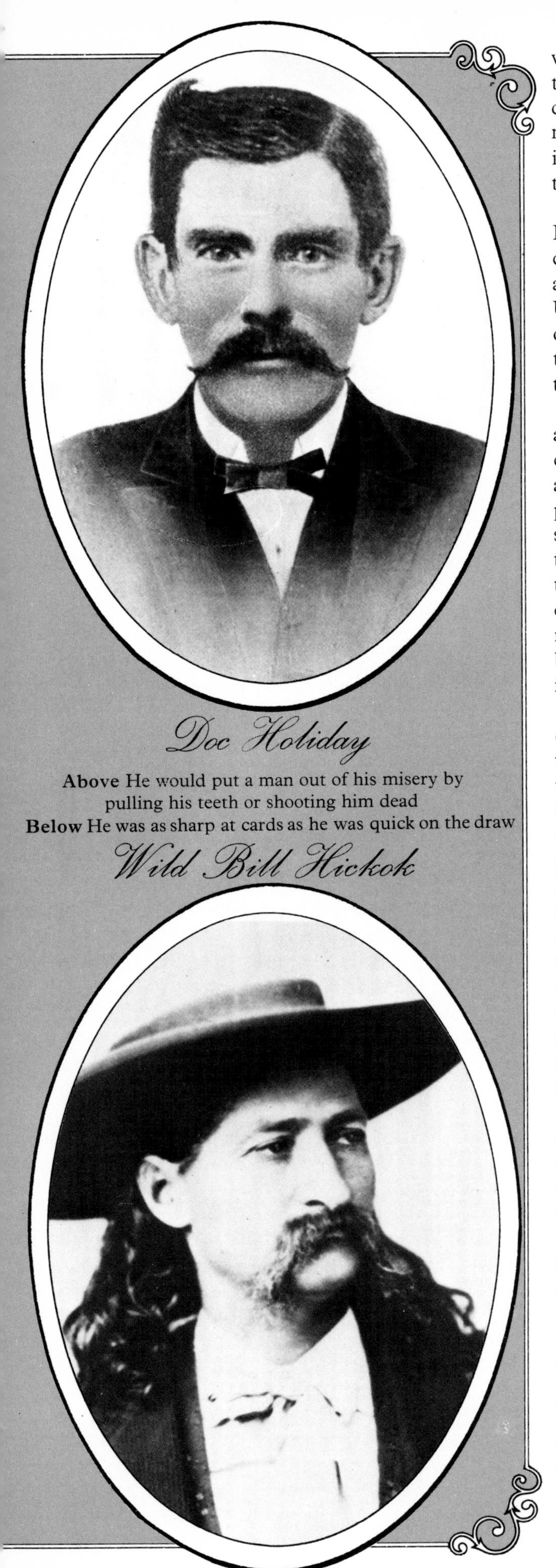

Doc Holiday

Above He would put a man out of his misery by pulling his teeth or shooting him dead
Below He was as sharp at cards as he was quick on the draw

Wild Bill Hickok

were caulked with tallow. These huge tubs were sometimes thirty feet in diameter and ten to twelve feet in depth. Usually two men with paddles and oars tried to manoeuver the ungainly craft. In fast currents and eddies it often spun crazily and was more often out of control than not.

As early as 1817, the steamboat *Pike* had reached St. Louis and three years later the *Western Engineer* churned up the muddy waters of the Missouri as far as Council Bluffs. The *Yellowstone* reached Fort Union in 1832, and in 1860 the *Key West* and *Chippewa* docked at Fort Benton, the head of, navigation. While the *Yellowstone* was a side wheeler, most boats plying the Missouri and its tributaries were stern wheelers.

The advantages of river travel were that great amounts of cargo and a sizable number of passengers could be transported inexpensively. But there were also dangers. Snags and sawyers were ever present to puncture the hulls, shifting currents caused hidden sandbars upon which the boats became grounded. All the boats were wood-burning and were often overstoked to get a higher head of steam. Greater speed, however, often meant burst boilers and fires. These accidents not only destroyed the cargo and ruined the consignor, but spoiled the trip completely for the passengers if it didn't blow them to bits.

The dream of a transcontinental railroad had increasingly excited the imagination of the nation as the western mining towns' wealth grew. By 1861, the vision was becoming a reality. In California, Mark Hopkins, Collis P. Huntington, Charles Crocker and Leland Stanford sank eight and a half million dollars into the dream. Together they formed the Central Pacific Railroad and a year later Congress granted them a charter. At the same time, the legislature appropriated money for the Union Pacific in the East. With the terminus at Omaha, the Union Pacific was to receive sixteen thousand dollars a mile for laying tracks. The Central Pacific could count on as much as forty-eight thousand dollars for putting down rails through some parts of the rough, mountainous stretches. The founders of the two railroad companies hedged against losses by forming contracting companies to receive the monies and complete the work. Crocker and Company, later the Contract and Finance Company, was the front for the Central Pacific. Stanford and his colleagues conveniently awarded themselves the contract. For the Union Pacific, the Credit Mobilier was set up and it feathered the nest of the eastern financiers in a similar manner.

At first progress was slow. In 1863 only forty miles had been completed. After the Civil War, however, the tracks began to stretch out from both West and East. Labor was a problem at the start, but this was solved by the Central Pacific's employment of hundreds upon hundreds of Chinese coolies. The Union Pacific hired an equal number of Irishmen. Tent cities sprang up all along the way. Every ten miles or so the grimy, bawdy rail towns with shacks for trollops and tents for saloons thrived on booze and gambling until the tracks had been laid for another stretch. Then the claptrap towns were dismantled, only to be re-established farther along the line. Some, like Cheyenne, became established and later served as centers of local commerce and trade. Others fell apart from dry rot, blown away by the winds of the high plains and rugged mountains.

In the early spring of 1869, six years after the first spikes had been driven, the two lines were fast approaching one another. Oddly, no one had given much thought as to where they would connect. And yet, not oddly at all. The backers of both companies were in the construction business. They were making fortunes in building railroads, not running them. Actually, few of the backers had any intention of operating the lines. That was a fool's gamble. Rather, they intended to sell out to the highest bidder.

So, to keep the money rolling in, the two lines didn't connect but passed each other. Appallingly, each continued running parallel to the other for a considerable distance. Congress, as usual bogged down in its self-congratulatory rhetoric confined chiefly to representing each politician's own self-interests, was somehow jarred into reality. On one of its historic occasions, Congress acted positively. It decided the railroads should meet and moreover connect at a specific place named Promontory Point in Utah.

On May 10, 1869, the two companies joined rails. Prayers were offered, speeches were made and the locomotive engineers shook hands. President Stanford of the Central Pacific and President Dillon of the Union joined forces in driving in the "Golden Spike" thus tying the nation together in one grand symbolic gesture. Stanford raised his sledge and with a masterful stroke aimed for the spike. Brilliantly, he flubbed it. His next stroke found him placing the head of the sledge gently on the spike. Dillon struck it neat and clean. And with this earth-shaking ceremony, the nation was as one, tied together with two ribbons of steel.

With the country joined, commerce could now flourish. Farmers and ranchers could get their produce to urban centers more quickly and more cheaply. The West would now fill up with people and towns. Prosperity would abound and law and order would prevail. The theory sounded fine and indeed worked beyond most men's fondest hopes. All, that is, except for law and order.

To say that law in the West was rudimentary would be a gross overstatement. Cattle rustlers, horse thieves, stagecoach robbers were commonplace. Nor were banks and trains immune to the outlaw's greed. Crime was always running rampant. What courts did exist were often poorly served by ill-trained judges. Skill in politics was always more valuable than a knowledge of jurisprudence. The result was that men frequently took the law into their own hands. To shoot first and ask questions later was a common practice, and the popular name "peacemaker" for the six-shooting revolver was not without reason.

If the cowboys were wild, the mining towns were roaring. Tombstone, Arizona, was as rough as any. Big

and wealthy, it attracted many miners as well as the usual crop of unsavory characters. It was here that Wyatt Earp made the OK Corral historic in just about one minute. Together with Doc Holliday and his own brothers Morgan and Virgil, who was marshall, he blasted to smithereens three cattle-rustling cowboys who threatened them. The victims died with their boots on and "Boot Hill" made a pleasant cemetery in the frying sun.

The list of the more infamous criminals is a long one. Books and biographical sketches fill library shelves. Many are highly romanticized and purport to make the outlaws some kind of heroes. Legion are the tales of urchins bullied into self-defense, good boys turned sour, courageous thieves robbing the rich to pay off a destitute widow's mortgage and save her starving children. In the 1880s and '90s, dime novels luridly portrayed the life and times of these desperados. The populace avidly absorbed the blood and thunder, the aggressive violence these cheap books purveyed. Schoolboys were caught reading these ghastly tales in haylofts and attics. Confiscated, fathers read them at night in the comfort of their Boston rocking chairs. The fact of the matter is, the bad men of the West were no good. There is no record of outlaws rescuing beleaguered widows. Rather, the road agents and the bank robbers spent the money they stole on themselves—for whiskey, women and for the fun of gambling. Nor is it quite necessary to kill thirty-seven men, as did Wess Hardin, to avenge a beating one once took at the hands of a bully.

While some of their exploits may be legendary, the outlaws themselves were real enough. Frank and Jesse James teamed up with the Younger brothers, Bob, Jim and Cole, to rob trains and banks. Billy the Kid, Sam Bass and Wesley Hardin were erstwhile cowboys specializing in murder. "Doc" Holliday was a cavernous consumptive, deputized by the Earps. His specialties were pulling teeth, playing cards and shooting men who accused him of cheating. Grat, Bob and Emmett Dalton were masterly train robbers. However, when they tried their hand at robbing two banks at the same time, the irate citizens of Coffeeville, Kansas, sent Grat and Bob to see their Maker and Emmett to the state peniten-

Far left Rest from toil. Bill Powers, Bob and Grat Walton and Dick Broadwell relax after trying to rob two banks at the same time
Left Rough justice for an outlaw. Steve Young was hanged by Vigilantes at Laramie in October 1868. "Necktie Parties" were quite a common occurrence in the West as the nearest lawman could be two days' ride away. Murderers and cattle rustlers could expect little mercy at the hands of an incensed mob determined that justice should be seen to be done and quickly too

tiary for life. And then there was the "Wild Bunch" led by "Butch" Cassidy. The gang held up banks and trains and stole cattle at will. Safe in the "Hole in the Wall," their hideaway in the mountains of Wyoming, "Butch" and the "Sun Dance Kid," the "Tall Texan," "Kid Curry" and others counted their loot.

In one way or another justice nearly always prevailed. If the outlaws didn't kill themselves in vendettas, the posses and the sheriffs did. Lynchings by outraged citizens often ended in hangings, and "necktie parties" drew crowds and gloating spectators. Sentences were often stiff and judges were quick to sentence a murderer or horse thief to be "hung by the neck until dead, dead, dead."

One of the severer ones was the dignified, overbearing, Bible-reading Isaac C. Parker. His stern justice sentenced to hanging eighty-eight men during his term of office, sometimes as many as four or five at a time. His punishments earned him the name of the "Hanging Judge." Judge Roy Bean was a different sort. Fat, uneducated and as genteel as a hog in a wallow, he moved West with the railroads. He finally stopped at a town called Langtry which he claimed to have been named in honor of Lillie, the darling of the English stage. Here he set up a saloon, got himself elected judge and held court in his barroom, He had three loves: convicting criminals, whiskey and Lillie. His law was pretty much off the cuff. Like too many jurists, he confused himself with God, and manipulated the law to suit his fancy. He went so far as to fine a corpse for what money was found on the body. It was a crime for even a dead man to carry a weapon. Nor was he adverse to sentencing a man to hang. A convenient tree which stood by his court served as an excellent gallows. But the best thing about Bean's trials was that his jurors could buy drinks at the bar before hearing each case. His first two loves were adequately fulfilled, but his last, the lovely Lillie Langtry, who unbelievably made the effort to visit her namesake, arrived in town eight months after the pudgy judge had died.

While the courts maintained a rough sort of justice, lawmen and detectives did their share. The names of Wyatt Earp, Bat Masterson and Pat Garrett fill the history books. As sleuths, none were more relentless than the Pinkertons. Cow towns employed lawmen to keep the peace. Abilene hired Tom Smith in 1870 to do the job at a hundred and fifty dollars a month. Smith promptly ordered that all firearms be banned in town and knocked down a ruffian named Hank when he defied the ruling. Later, Wyoming Frank wanted to keep his guns, but got pushed into a bar by Smith. The sheriff took his arms as he was down. The citizens of Abilene raised Smith's pay by seventy-five dollars forthwith.

Wild Bill Hickok came to Abilene after Smith was murdered by a vicious settler named McConnell who chopped off Smith's head in a quarrel. Hickok had considerable reputation as a gunman. He proved it at the expense of the criminal element and those who crossed him. He once modestly admitted to having killed over a hundred men, a record which earned him the title of Hero of the West. In Abilene he spent most of his time gambling in a saloon and kept the peace as much by his reputation as by his skill with side arms. After less than a year, Hickok's contract was allowed to lapse and so did his career. He drifted about the country and ended up in the mining town of Deadwood, South Dakota. Here, as he was playing cards, he was shot in the back by courageous Jack McCall for no better reason than that he wanted to wipe out a superior gunman. This was on August 2, 1876. Hickok was forty-nine years old, a ripe age for a lawman in those days.

The conquering of the American West would appear to have been the accomplishment of daring explorers and flamboyant military men, of willful and lustful entrepreneurs, of robber barons and outright brigands. But that's not quite so. It was really accomplished by a very stalwart and determined people. Most were law-abiding, hardworking, God-fearing citizens. In addition to farmers and doctors, lawyers and ranchers, their ranks included all categories of endeavor—preachers and schoolteachers, blacksmiths and bankers, coopers and shopkeepers. They were the followers, the good, dependable souls, the "salt of the earth." Their lives were often as drab and dull as they were conforming. Rarely did they make the headlines in the annals of history. And yet it was they, with their simplistic view of life, who would prove to be the effective subduers of the West. Their contribution, while neither sensational nor profound, was in fact solid and sustained. As such, it is truly they who made the West a valuable and integral part of an expanding and prosperous nation.

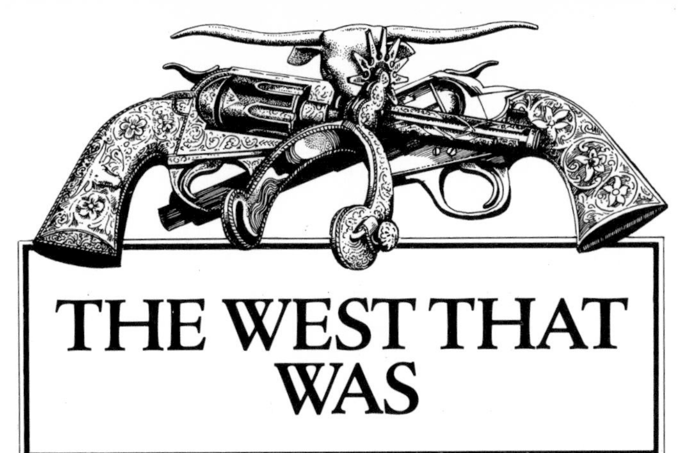

THE WEST THAT WAS

The early West is now immortalized in countless books and movies: one of the earliest attempts to popularize the West being Buffalo Bill's Wild West Show. Today parts of the West are protected as National Parks where one can go in search of the West that was.

Left Turning the clock back is becoming a popular way of spending a weekend

BY THE TURN of the twentieth century, the West of the wild Indians and resolute explorers, the pioneers, the trappers, the novice miners and the Longhorn drovers was pretty much a memory. No one date can mark the end of this fabulous era, but arbitrarily 1900 is as good a one as any. Well before that, however, men were already romanticizing the past glories in fiction and art and capitalizing on it through their own experiences or those of others.

Among the writers to popularize the West were such men as Owen Wistar and Zane Grey, Emerson Hough, Charles Siringo and Will James. The list is much longer. Owen Wistar was a Philadelphia lawyer who came West for his health. His novel, *The Virginian*, published in 1902, won him immediate fame. As a best seller, it brought the aura of the West to the eastern public in a heroic manner which no one before had quite achieved. Zane Grey was a prolific and melodramatic writer who turned out reams of books. Often fanciful and sometimes improbable, his *Riders of the Purple Sage* was to become his most popular. Emerson Hough wrote novels of the West and was a serious scholar. His *Covered Wagon* published in 1922 and *North of 36* printed the following year were two of his best. Charles Siringo, a former trail hand and ex-sheriff wrote narratives and a history of the West based largely on his own experiences. Will James, like Siringo, was himself a cowboy and he wrote from firsthand knowledge. His poignant story of the cowpony, *Smoky*, is enhanced by his own sketches.

Many writers and artists who extolled the West with pen and brush were in fact easterners attracted by its glamour. Charles Marion Russell, though born in St. Louis in 1864, almost qualifies as an indigenous westerner. Son of a prominent family, his father was not only a Yale graduate but president of a large brick company. Charles's early interest, however, was directed neither toward education nor business. As a boy he devoted his energies to playing Indians and trappers in the woods and filling his schoolbooks with sketches of wildlife. To help redirect their son's interest into a proper and acceptable academic career, his parents sent Charles to a military school in Burlington, New Jersey. This lasted about six months. Instead of making his marks, he spent most of his time doing guard duty as a disciplinary measure. When he returned to St. Louis, his parents conceded his artistic talent and sent him to art school. He lasted there three days. In the desperate hope of getting the spell of the West out of the boy's system, his father agreed to a western trip. A friend of the family, "Pike" Miller, was part owner of a sheep ranch in Montana and he agreed to take on Charlie. At the age of sixteen, the boy could tend sheep on the Judith Basin.

Charlie stayed on at the Miller Ranch for about a year and he made a lot of sketches. He also lost a lot of sheep and got himself fired. With not much else to do, he spent a winter with the Blackfeet Indians. Later, with even less to do, he was given shelter by a hunter named Jake Hoover who took pity on him. Charlie spent a year at Jake's cabin making drawings of the wild world around him. More by luck than intention Charlie then hired on as a horse wrangler for a cattle roundup. He did his job well and soon was responsible for two hundred cow ponies. For eleven years Charlie worked as a wrangler, a cowpuncher and a ranch hand. And all the time he made drawings, sketches and paintings of what he saw. The cowboys approved his work. Charlie drew it like it was.

The winter of 1886 was what cattlemen call a "cow killer." It was the year of the great blizzard which engulfed the Plains. When the spring thaws came, thousands upon thousands of carcasses were all that remained of once great herds. The owner of the OK Ranch, trying to write to a friend describing how his cattle had fared, noticed that Charlie was drawing a picture on a small piece of cardboard. The owner tore up his letter and mailed instead Charlie's postcard-sized sketch titled *Waiting for a Chinook*. His friend got the message.

Charlie kept on drawing. In 1888, *Harper's Weekly* published his picture *Caught in the Act*. With that, after eleven years of cowboying, Charlie gave it up to devote full time to recording the West. In 1893 he moved to Great Falls, selling his paintings now and again, some

to a family friend in St. Louis, some to Sid Willis, owner of the Mint Bar. Charlie thought a price of twenty-five dollars was fair enough.

Already Charlie was a character. To his cowboy friends, his pictures were just right. They could pick out a particular horse, identify a well-known critter at a glance. That made the pictures good. Besides, his stories of cowboying rang true, his sense of humor was dry and telling. Wearing his old boots and a red sash at his waist, he was a welcome addition at any bar.

In Great Falls, Charlie was introduced to a girl from Kentucky named Nancy Cooper. Nancy, only seventeen, was enamored of this thirty-nine-year-old cowboy and his paintings and a year later Charlie and Nancy were married. Nancy was also interested in helping her husband market his paintings to better advantage. She did this in two ways. First she was able to convince Charlie not to spend most of the day at the bar with his drinking cronies, so he painted all morning and visited with his friends in the afternoons, limited to two drinks. Second, she was able to find more buyers for his paintings at increased prices.

It was in 1911 that his first one-man show was held in New York. By now, Charlie Russell, the cowboy artist, was nationally recognized. In 1914 his works were shown twice in London. And with his cowboy hat, boots and red sash, he cut quite a figure.

As the years passed, Charlie turned out hundreds upon hundreds of sketches and paintings, many as illustrations for popular magazines of the day. To his repertoire he added sculpture, these works possessing the same verve and simple freshness as his paintings. Nancy, too, was entirely successful in getting increasingly good prices for his work. In 1921 he received ten thousand dollars for a rather small painting. Commissioned in 1926 by a well-to-do Californian for a picture to fill a special place, Charlie charged thirty thousand dollars.

Charles Russell loved the West he had known as a young man. For him, the nesters with their plows and barbed wire, the vanishing buffalo and the reservation Indians were a sad commentary on a once free and wild West. Russell's works were an attempt to preserve what was no more and in achieving this goal he was indeed both skilled and faithful.

Frederic Remington, unlike Russell, was a product of the Ivy League. A graduate of the Yale School of Fine Arts, he had a passion for both painting and the West. At the age of nineteen he made his first trip to Montana, chiefly to get the taste of it. He also made many sketches. Two years later, in 1883, he spent his modest inheritance on a small sheep ranch in Kansas. This was hardly the wild West, but the experience gave him a stern backdrop for his later work.

Deciding to devote full time to art, Remington sold his ranch a year later. He moved to Kansas City, married his New York sweetheart and began work in earnest. As the years passed, Remington became prolific. His illustrations of Indians, cowboys and the U.S. Cavalry appeared in all the more popular magazines. He traveled widely throughout the West carefully studying costumes and equipment to ensure the accuracy of his work. Overall, his diligence produced some twenty-seven hundred paintings and drawings and twenty-two bronzes.

In 1891, before he was thirty, he was elected an associate member of the National Academy of Design, an honor he much coveted. Like Russell's, his portrayals of Indian warfare and cavalry engagements were impressions of events that had happened earlier. This, however, in no way lessened their appeal nor Remington's contribution to the telling of the West's history which he so respected. His career was cut short by a combination of obesity and an acute appendicitis. Before the surgeon could knife through the blubber, peritonitis set in. He died at the age of forty-eight.

One of the most spectacular promoters of the bygone days was the former Pony Express rider, army scout and buffalo hunter, William Cody, known throughout the world as "Buffalo Bill." His career as a showman began on a New York stage in 1872. The play *Buffalo Bill, King of the Border Men* was drawing enthusiastic crowds at the time. At one performance Buffalo Bill himself was in the audience. Spotted by the promoter, Ned Buntline, he was brought to the stage where he was loudly acclaimed and was immediately stagestruck.

Below Relic of a vanished age. Cattle graze near the ghost town of Bodie, California

Cody's popularity as a hero of the West was not without merit. His career began at the age of fifteen as a Pony Express rider, a job requiring endurance and courage few men are asked to match. Later he served as chief of scouts for the Fifth Cavalry. In an engagement with the Cheyenne, he successfully rescued two couriers and gained fame with the killing of a young chief, Yellow Hand. Employed by the Kansas Pacific Railroad in 1868 to supply meat for the construction gangs, he is credited with killing over four thousand buffalo in the short period of a year and a half. For this bit of mass butchery, he earned the name Buffalo Bill.

After Cody's initial appearance in New York, Buntline gave him a part in a new play, *Scout of the Plains*, and the showman in him emerged. Not until 1883, however, did the famous Wild West Show make its début. Opening in Omaha, its success was meteoric. Now the public could witness firsthand live buffalo, real Indians attacking the stage, genuine cowboys displaying feats of horsemanship and steer roping. Even the celebrated gunslinger Wild Bill Hickok was on display shooting up the arena. Cody himself led the charging procession on a white steed. Dressed in buckskins and a big hat and with his white hair flowing, he was a dashing and colorful figure. As an excellent marksman, together with the beloved Annie Oakley he shot glass balls from the air. Annie even shot cigarettes from her trusting husband's lips. All in all it was a noisy "shoot-em-up" show and everyone loved it. Cody took his show to England in 1887, two command performances being given for the Queen. Later he toured Europe where his popularity soared.

For all his bombast, egotism and showmanship, Cody was a poor businessman. This, combined with his heavy drinking, led to the show's decline. 1910 was the last good year and seven years later Cody died destitute. They buried him on Look Out Mountain near Denver.

The artists' portrayals, the writers' dramatizations and the historians' factual recordings have preserved much of the West as it was. But today its rugged character has been transformed into one of safe and soft gentility. It is as though a chemist had converted strong whiskey into lukewarm tea. The vastness of the Plains still remains, it is true, the grandeur of the lofty mountains and the brilliance of the western sunsets still inspire awe. Deer and elk, black bears and grizzlys may yet be found in wilderness areas. Coyotes still prey on sheep, and antelope roam the Plains. And here and there hawks and eagles wheel high above the blue horizon as beavers build their dams in cool wooded streams far below. But their numbers have been decimated and their habitats severely reduced. Buffalo and a handful of wolves are confined to preserves. The wilds that once were the West are now very tame indeed.

The West was destined for exploitation. At first it was the trappers who depleted the beaver. They were followed by the miners scarring the hills for gold and silver. Settlers from the East felled the forests and broke the sod. Later, men grazed their cattle and sheep on the free grass. Within seventy-five years, the seemingly inexhaustible resources were running out. No longer was it profitable to mine the precious metals. The discovery of rich coal and oil deposits in the later part of the nineteenth century did add a new dimension to the country's wealth, yet within a century they too were severely drained. Not until the 1930s did farmers and ranchers practice sound conservation techniques. Prior to that, much range was damaged by overgrazing, wind erosion caused great dust storms in sodded regions which should never have been plowed. Strangely, even the agriculturalists who represent the chief contributors to a true production economy, were overzealously destroying the very resource upon which their life depended. Like the farmers, the lumbermen, after nearly destroying their rich resource, finally began the practice of cutting on a sustained yield basis combined with a program of reforestation.

Now, in the last quarter of the twentieth century, westerners are still exploiting their country. Cursed by overpopulation, misled by the falacious philosophy that because things are bigger they are better, and duped by the insidious theory that only through growth can an economy function, the inhabitants have gone far to destroy the beauties and threaten the riches of the West. A combination of factors have played interlocking parts to bring this about.

A rapid growth in population has strained housing facilities of many western communities. Much of this growth has been promoted by state governments and chambers of commerce frantically seeking new industries to expand economic productivity and increase the tax base. Real estate developers have been quick to capitalize on the ever-expanding urban sprawl by buying up parcel upon parcel of valuable agricultural land at prices ranchers and farmers cannot afford to reject. As a result, many productive agricultural areas are all too

rapidly being displaced by an unproductive and not very attractive suburbia.

Water has always been at a premium in the West. Water rights have been jealously guarded and theoretically protected by law. The vast amounts of water required by new industry and an expanding population have placed the supply at a dangerously low level. Water tables drop, demanding deeper and deeper wells, more and larger dams. Proponents of these gigantic reservoirs claim various benefits including hydroelectric power, increased irrigation, flood control and added recreational facilities for fishermen and boating enthusiasts. The engineers who design these monsters, however, fail in their cost-benefit calculations to foresee their eventual uselessness through silting. Instead, advocates lobby for another boondoggle. Not only do these reservoirs destroy irreplaceable farmland and wildlife habitats, but untold natural beauty. As recently as 1974, government planners were demanding the obliteration of an impressive natural bridge on the Colorado River by backing water into the Grand Canyon of Arizona. None of these engineers has foresight enough to figure the cost and practicality of draining and dredging silt from their unsightly constructions. They prefer to build more monuments to men's engineering achievements at the expense of nature's beauty. In the event, the shortsighted dam builders have been entirely successful in spoiling much of the western landscape.

The West has long held a spell for adventurers and the twentieth century has been no exception. Today the tourist, the vacationer and the dude can pile his wife and kids in the car and savor the wonders of a bygone day. The westerners are quite realistic about this state of affairs, for they know the gold that once was in those hills is now in the tourists' pockets. For the well-to-do, the dude ranch offers a chance to play cowboy, to spend a week or more riding the range with real wranglers and singing cowboy songs around a campfire. The national parks offer natural wonders—geysers and wild animals, Indian ruins and forests of petrified trees. Associated with the parks are all manner of camping and motel accomodation, cafeterias and gasoline stations to attract thousands of visitors and make their stay a pleasant one. Concessionaires get rich selling food and supplies, cheap novelties and gimcracks. All this is superficially proper and fitting. The American public has every right to the recreational and educational advantages these great parks offer. But what is not fitting and proper is that the hordes of humanity clogging the roads with their cars and touring buses have thoroughly spoiled any sense of natural beauty the parks might once have possessed. People's comfort and safety have quite understandably taken precedence in view of the wild nature of the animals and dangers inherent in visiting many of the natural wonders, but emphasis on comfort and safety has reached ridiculous proportions. Recently two incidents occurred in Yellowstone National Park in Wyoming which indicate the utter disregard for ecological considerations. The gorgeous hot pools in the park can be visited easily by following well-marked boardwalks. Signs warn tourists of the dangers and the need to remain on the walks. But when a wayward child, whose parents were gawking at something else, stupidly fell into one of the pools and was seriously scalded, people began demanding that the pools be fenced. When two willful young men deliberately camped in an area plainly marked as off limits and one was mauled to death by a grizzly bear, maudlin park rangers with a warped sense of justice shot the bear. In trying to be all things to all people, park authorities have succumbed to the outdated approach that the greater the number they attract, the better they serve the public good. If, how-

Left The West today. Dude ranch riders in Colorado's Rocky Mountains
Below Pony chuck wagon racing—a colorful and exciting rodeo event

ever, the parks and their wonders are to be preserved, restrictions such as limiting the number of visitors by requiring reservations should be instituted. As matters stand, not only are the parks being worn out, but they are about as appealing as rush hour on a Manhattan subway.

Sportsmen, too, do their share in destroying the environment. Surprisingly, the hunters and fishermen are probably the best controlled. Quotas are placed on most wild game so that, for example, only specified numbers of deer, elk and antelope may be shot. But there are those men who love to kill just for the sport with no intention of eating their quarry, while there are many others who evade the wardens, either shooting animals out of season or in numbers beyond the legal limit. Today more and more animals—the grizzly bear, the mountain lion, the golden eagle—are being placed on the endangered list.

Despite the onslaught of too many people and the inevitable forces of progress and change, there are a growing number of men and women working to retain something of the quality of the nation's western heritage. Groups have formed to restore historic landmarks and preserve natural wonders. Ecologically concerned organizations are active in developing wildlife preserves and sponsoring statutes for the protection of endangered species. Their endeavors supplement federal and state programs for wilderness areas, parks, monuments and shrines as well as the activities of local and state historical societies. This is good, but the flavor and character of the West is not to be achieved in pickling history. Rather, it is to be found in the attitude of its people.

Today, there are still Indians, and while no longer buffalo-hunting warriors, they are regaining a pride in their heritage and properly demanding their rightful place as proud contributors within the nation. There are still miners seeking riches, albeit many are technically trained in specialized universities to supervise sophisticated mining operations. There are still cattlemen trying to make money running working ranches, and cowboys branding calves with red-hot irons. And there are rodeos where tough men ride bucking broncos and "bulldog" steers to the thrill of applauding spectators. The road agents holding up stagecoaches have vanished, but bank robbers and cattle rustlers still ply their professions. Sheriffs still get paid to wear badges and hunt down criminals. The smooth-talking horse traders are now used-car dealers. Sadly the judges no longer keep bars. Today the West has all the characteristics of civilized society. Its cities of skyscrapers, its handsome churches, its fine museums and libraries and great universities are the attributes of culture for which the westerners have striven. Regrettably, in so doing, they have made the West just like every other place. And yet, for all of this, the West still makes its mark. And it has done it for the westerners in a very simple, a very beautiful way. When parting company, instead of saying "Good night" or "Goodbye" or "So long" or "See you later," an astonishing number of westerners say, "Have a nice day." And they mean it!

Below Cowboys driving Longhorns through Old Tuscan village

INDEX

Page numbers in *italics* denote illustrations

ACKNOWLEDGEMENTS

The publishers would like to thank the following individuals and organizations for their kind permission to reproduce the pictures in this book:

Arizona State Historical Society 96 right. *Barnabys* 120–121, 122–123, 125, 126. *Bizzell Library, University of Oklahoma, Norman, Oklahoma* 117 above. *Boatman's National Bank, St. Louis* 28–29 above. *Butler Institute of American Art* 2–3. *Camera Press* 104–105. *Amon Carter Museum of Western Art, Fort Worth, Texas* 46–47, 78, 82, 83 above, 83 below, 90 above 91 above. *Cincinnati Art Museum* 74–75. *Colorado State Historical Society* 4–5. *Corcoran Gallery, Washington DC* 16 above left, 16 above right *Denver Public Library* 9, 16 below, 17 left, 22–23 below, 32, 38, 39 above left, 39 below, 43 right, 48 left, 59, 62, 64 above, 69 below right, 76, 76 inset, 78–79, 86–87, 92 left, 96 left, 96 center, 97 left, 97 right, 101, 103 left, 110 right, 117 below, 118 and back jacket. *The Detroit Institute of Arts* 26–27 below. *Mary Evans Picture Library* 12 left, 72. *Gilcrease Institute of History & Art, Tulsa, Oklahoma* 27 above, 60–61, 94–95. *R. B. Hassrick* 6–7, 14–15 center. *Annie Horton* 24 left, 52–53. *Nina Hull Miller, Lexington, Nebraska* 119. *Idaho Historical Society* 109 below right. *International Harvester Company, New York* 107. *J. Jerome Hill Reference Library, St. Maul, Minnesota* 42–43 center below, 73. *Joseph G. Rosa*, front flap. *Kansas State Historical Society, Topeka, Kansas* 32–33, 85, 88–89, 92–93 below, 116 below. *Library of Congress* 88 below. *Ruth Koerner Oliver* 87 below and back jacket. *J. Maxwell Moran Collection, Time Inc., New York City* 70–71 *above*. *McMillan Company, New York* 11 above. *Metropolitan Museum of Art, New York City* 6 left. *Minnesota Historical Society* 68–69 above. *Missouri Historical Society* 30, 31 above. *Montana Historical Society* 99, 114–115 and back flap. *Museum of New Mexico, Sante Fe* 97 center. *National Gallery of Canada* 14 left. *Nebraska Historical Society* 64–65 below. *New Briton Museum of American Art* 11 below. *New York Historical Society* 16 above center. *New York Public Library* 31 below, 42–43 above. *Nevada Historical Society* 103 below. *North Carolina Museum of History* 57. *Oklahoma State Historical Society* 98. *Oregon Historical Society* 57. *Peabody Museum, Harvard* 40 below left. *Pennsylvania Academy of Fine Arts* 37, 58 above. *Public Archives of Canada* 58 below. *Royal Ontario Museum, Toronto* 23 above. *The St. Louis Art Museum* 34 left, 52 left. *The St. Louis Color Postcard Co.* 17 right. *Carl Shaefer Dentzel* 28 below. *Shelburne Museum Inc., Shelburne, Vermont* 62–63. *Smithsonian Institute, Washington DC* 12 right, 34–35, 39 above right, 40–41, 44, 45, 49, 102. *Taft Museum, Cincinnati* 50–51. *Mrs J. Tadd Moore* 90–91 below. *Union Pacific Railway* 100–101. *U.S. Forest Service* 112–113 above. *U. S. National Archives* 49 right, 116 above, 118. *University of Michigan, Museum of Art* 66–67 and front jacket. *University of Oregon* 93 above. *Utah State Historical Society* 68–69 below, 105. *Wadsworth Athenaeum, Hartford, Connecticut* 15 right. *Walters Art Gallery* 20–21, 24 right. *Washington University Gallery of Art, St. Louis* 10, 54–55. *Wells Fargo Bank* 108–109 below, 110 left, 111. *West Point Museum Collections* 13. *Western Americana* 8–9, 20 left, 26 above, 88 above, 106 above, 106 below, 108–109 above, 109 above right, 112 left, 112 below right, 121 right, 124. *Western Americana/Yale University Library* 25. *Whitney Gallery of Western Art, Cody, Wyoming* 80–81. *Woolaroc Museum, Bartlesville, Oklahoma* 48–49, 70 below. *Yale University Library* 69 below left.

The Amer

VAN COUVER Is.
WASHINGTON
Astoria
Fort Clatsop
WHITMAN MISSION
OREGON
Oregon Trail
IDAHO
SHOSHONI
BLACKFEET
Great Falls of the Missouri
MONTANA
Fort Benton
CROW
Virginia City
Bozeman Trail
Custer's Last Stand
Yellowstone
Buffalo
Fort Kearny
Popo Agie
SIOUX
N. DAKOTA
MANDAN VILLAGES
ARIKARA
Mount Rushmore
S. DAKOTA
Fort Pierre
Wounded Knee
Fort Laramie
NEBRASKA
Promontory Point
California Trail
South Pass
Cheyenne
PAWNEE
Sutter's Fort
Donner's Disaster
Sacramento
San Francisco
NEVADA
Salt Lake City
ARAPAHO
Denver
Central Overland Road
Leadville
Russell's Gold Find
COLORADO
KANSAS
Abilene
CALIFORNIA
UTAH
UTES
Pikes Peak
CHEYENNE
Bent's Fort
Dodge City
Santa Fe Trail
NAVAHO
NEW MEXICO
Taos
ARIZONA
ZUNI
Sante Fé
Cimarron Cut-off
KIOWA
Western Trail
Chisholm Trail
SKY CITY
Lincoln
Yuma
APACHE
COMANCHE
Tombstone
El Paso
Butterfield Overland Mail
Langtry
The Alamo